PRAYER *for* BUSY PEOPLE

a simple guide to life-changing prayer

By Jamie Tyrrell

Published by
Vital Faith Resources
P.O. Box 18378
Pittsburgh, PA 15236
412-655-4958
www.vitalfaithresources.com

ISBN 978-1-931551-10-6

Dedication

To my wife, Bessie: In pondering our relationship
I have often met the face of God's love.

*"The pursuit of wisdom especially joins man to
God in friendship."*

Thomas Aquinas[1]

---

1 Thomas Aquinas, *Summa Comtra Gentiles* (N□w Yo□k: Doub□□day, 1955). Th□s□ a□□ his fi□s□ wo□ds,
which a□□ found on □h□ f□y□□af b□fo□□ □h□ □□x□ b□gins.

Table of Contents

Acknowledgements

I am grateful for so many people. Ben Johnson, the former Director of Evangelism for the Presbyterian Church in the United States and retired Professor of Spirituality at Columbia Theological Seminary, founded the Certificate of Spirituality Program out of Columbia Seminary. That program introduced me to many of the historic saints of the church and contemporary practitioners of the art of prayer.

Through the program I also met E. Stanley Ott, who led a seminar on church growth. He asked each one of us what ministry we would invest our lives in if we were bold. When it was my turn, I said that I would like to encourage people to engage the richness of the presence of God. I thought it might be helpful to publish a book about Christian meditation. Stan said that Ben Johnson had just given him a publishing house and he was looking for authors. He offered me his friendship, arranged for editors and a publisher. My breath was taken away. How God surprises us!

I am indebted to Alec Sutherland, Robert Tyrrell, Jane Hope, Larry Iwan, Don and Rachel Rensberger, Roy and Jill Snyder, Jim and Marcia Torpey, Dick and Mary Lou Havens and Bruce and Cindy Anderson. They have read manuscripts, made suggestions, listened to me struggle to find words and allowed me the privilege of participating in their lives. Numerous other students have sometimes caused me to ponder, taught me or encouraged me. In a sense, this book is the product of a multitude.

My editors have been wonderful. Rev. Karen Berns read the original shambles and gave me a good start. Rev. Dr. Rachel Stahle helped in so many ways, but especially in broadening my audience. Marianne Holohan's eye for structure has made this work much more readable. Since I am a "whole idea" sort of person, Pam Volk's eye for detail has been a terrific help. Stuart Hoffman made many suggestions to make the book more readable and interesting. The page maker and graphic editor, Tim Kostilnik, has worked wonders. Once again, thank you all.

Introduction

A new command I give you: Love one another.
As I have loved you, so you must love one
another (John 13:34).

We honor Jesus the Christ when we learn to love others with his love. Until we learn that, everything is preparation. The enemy of learning is undisciplined hurry.

It is not just that we have things to do. Our internal life is frantic. The busyness of our own souls is not an accident. I called a 92-year-old housebound woman to set up a visit. She announced, proudly, that she was far too busy today. She had a doctor's appointment. I would have to call another time. I was taken aback by the tone of her voice. She was positively excited to be able to say, "No." Being busy meant that she was still important.

There are other issues that drive busyness. Some people have never learned the art of slowing their thoughts so that they can hear and reflect on the conversation of their own hearts. Still others are careless about their surroundings. The clutter within reflects the clutter around them. Whatever the cause, the effect is the same. Until we cope with the endless mental activity of our own souls, we are trapped on our life's surface. We gain little or no practical wisdom from living. Eventually we become tired and irritated at life.

Meditation engages our inner self with God. It is a deeper, richer listening which leads to wisdom. It is the discipline that suspends busyness in favor of pondering the depths of life. It has always been necessary for a deep relationship with God. The psalmist wrote that those who live a blessed life stop in the midst of their busyness:

> *"and on his (God's) law he meditates day and*
> *night"* (Psalm 1:2b).

Jesus went aside to pray regularly. He also meditated. Matthew 6:25-30 records three meditations Jesus taught that address the spiritual problem of worry.

The method I offer is based on Solomon's prayer for wisdom. Early in his reign Solomon saw a vision of God. God offered to grant him any one wish. Solomon asked for "a God-listening heart" (1 Kings 3:9 TM). Many translations of his request say either "understanding" or "wisdom." The literal translation of the Hebrew is "a listening heart." In his paraphrase of the Bible called *The Message*, Eugene Peterson adds the word "God." I think that he is right on target and that the result is profound. From this perspective, Solomon's request can be seen as a request to listen for the heart of God, listen with a heart that is like God's and listen for the heart of the matter.

This method of meditation teaches you to listen for God. If you learn to listen, you can live the new command to love others with the love you meet in Jesus Christ.

To learn to listen is vital. Various surveys indicate that though as many as 87 percent of Americans pray at least weekly, over 50 percent of the population never take the time to listen. In other words, only about a third of us search our hearts for God's leading. Come and learn to listen for God. Join in the flow of the Spirit. The Christian life is wonderful, full of deep relationships, loyal friends, the courage to take risks, comfort in failure and exhilaration in success. Learn firsthand the character of God. Gain a fundamental peace and the blessing of an expectation of eternal joy at death.

The plan of this book is simple. It is written so that it can be used as a group session with a designated leader, or you can lead yourself through it. To lead a group, you will find the directions you need in the margin. When used in private, you can ignore the group leader's directions as you become familiar with the process. Instructions for individual use that require action are in the body of the text in *bold italic font*.

The first section of each week teaches a basic skill related to meditating, then offers a cycle of exercises that focus on some aspect of God's love. That cycle will help you sort out which voices inside your own soul may speak God's truth and which ones cannot. Starting at week three, I will encourage you to also think about the spirit behind a possible act of ministry. Jesus wants us to become wise in our actions towards others (Mt. 10:6).

After the cycle of exercises comes a section called Going Deeper that is designed to answer questions and stimulate thought. It will help you relate what you are learning to your experience. Many people find it more practical to do the first section in the morning and work through the Going Deeper section in the evening. Others do both at once. It is entirely up to you. I do encourage you to use both portions of each week's material.

There are several different types of material in the Going Deeper section. Usually there is an example of the results of a meditation on Scripture. You will also find spiritual principles illustrated out of my own experience or that of other people. I hope my little stories help you find God's presence in your life. Finally, there are short discussions addressing common questions. There will be four or five of these stories and discussions each week. You will find questions to help you ponder and to share.

The Appendixes include forms that you may find useful: God Sightings, Memos from God, Review of the Week and Prayer List.

A Proposition: Make a Commitment to Continue

Work through the seven weeks of prayers, then ask yourself these questions:

"Have these exercises made a difference in how I treat other people?"
"Am I more aware of God's activity?"
"Am I more thankful?"

Then ask:

"Based on my experience with these exercises, will I become a disciple (disciplined one) seeking a God-listening heart by reading from the Bible, meditating, praying for others and seeking God's leading in my daily life?"

I hope your answers are yes. God would like to be counted among your friends, in fact to be your best friend. God has promised to be with you to celebrate the victories of your life and to sit beside you in comfort when you deal with hard issues. God would like to be a guide when you are perplexed and to encourage you to love the people around you.

Leading a Group

If you are a group leader, you will find this program to be very flexible. Because it teaches a process, it can be shortened or stretched to fit your schedule. If you decide to drop one or more chapters, keep chapters one, six and seven as the core. On the other hand, you can use Paul's list of the attributes of love in 1 Corinthians 13 to extend the study. Keep in mind that a great deal of research shows that it takes a minimum of six weeks to establish a new habit. In the course of six weeks, most people will miss a meeting. Since this book is about developing a habit of meditation, it has seven chapters. After finishing the seventh week, have a dinner together. Relax and enjoy your fellowship. Then, return to the proposition above and discuss whether or not you are prepared to make a commitment to read the Bible, pray for others and listen for God's leading on a daily basis.

For some this book will be a life-changing experience. For others, it will be a mystery. Offer the Commitment as an aid for those who have found meditation meaningful. Make sure that those who do not relate to this form of prayer feel free to say so.

You are taking your group through a learning process. The goal is for them to learn to use meditation on their own. The leader's directions are in the margin. Directions for group members or individuals leading themselves through this study are in the body of the text in **bold italic font**. When the directions say "Pause," repeat the thought silently to yourself, then count to 15 slowly. If a number of people in your group say they sense no response to the prayers, try counting to 20 or even 30. If most are sensing a response and you have one or two who are not, encourage them to try at home. There they can take the time they need.

When the directions say to wait two minutes or three minutes, you may want to use a clock. Though these timeframes actually are not much time for a person trying to complete the exercises, it may seem like a long time to you.

If you have highly analytical people in your group or extreme introverts, they will want to mull over things and write copious notes. Encourage them to be brief. We all forget most of our daily experience and that is fine. Even years later the important moments remain vivid. A few key words are all that people need to remember important turning points.

If they allow themselves to learn to trust the Spirit, their reward will be tremendous. Trusting the Spirit allows us to be free from the tyranny of analyzing everything and to be free to focus on the important. They just might learn to love this type of prayer.

Welcome to the adventure! God will use this time to bless people through you. What a privilege we have to serve such a God.

Week One:
Lord, Do You Love Me?

Before you start, turn to Appendix A and make copies of the form called God Sightings. Turn to Appendix B and put the suggested headings on index cards. Have something to write with.

Leaders, make copies for your group.

Repeat each thought to yourself silently. Then be still and listen. Perhaps you will become aware of the Living God within. Let us pray:

Say,

"Present Lord, we offer you our hearts. Come and enter in. Help us to sort out the dialogue of our hearts. Help us to seize on your truth in the flood of words, images and impressions within us. In Christ's name. Amen."

Pause.
Say,

You are loved. This week you will learn how to use meditation to be immediately aware of God's love for you. You will also begin to practice a powerful way to make Jesus' new command, "Love others as God loves you" (John 13:34b), the foundation of your life.

Meditation addresses the fact that most people live lives that are too busy. It is not that we are too active. We are meant to be active. That is how God created us. Being too busy is another matter. We know the difference by its effect on us. When people are appropriately active, they become

If in a group, take turns reading.

1

stronger and joyful. When they are too busy, they become depleted.

The practice of meditation is simpler than you may think. In fact, you already meditate. Common secular words for meditation are "to consider my options," "to worry" and "to daydream." In this book you will learn how to focus the intelligence of your heart on your relationship to God and to others. You will have the opportunity to practice.

The first exercise is based on Psalm 23. It helps most people create a quiet space in the center of their activities. Feel free to use it anytime.

The first cycle of exercises has you do three things. First, you review your awareness of how God has loved you in the past. Second, you focus on your recent experience of God's love. Third, you prepare yourself to intentionally love another with Christ's love.

The Going Deeper section follows. I encourage you to pick one subject a day to chew on. You may want to work on it at a different time each day.

Once you have completed this cycle, I think you will begin to see how this book can help you make Jesus' new command the active foundation of your life. Because you are taking time to consider your experience, you will begin to develop practical Christian wisdom. Your personal ministry will flourish. You will be blessed as you bless others.

General Information on Meditation

To know God's love each of us has to find effective
ways to be aware of it. The Hebrew word *hagah*
is often translated as "meditate." It means "to
murmur like a brook." In Psalm 119 the author uses
the word *siyach* which means to "mutter to ourselves." In the New Testament, Matthew uses the
word *emblepho* meaning literally "to look at in-
tently" with the connotation of "until you learn the
lesson thoroughly." It can also be translated as
"meditate."

Meditation is an activity of what the Bible calls our
"hearts" or "inner selves." In our hearts we relate
our experience and our faith to specific actions. We
also decide whether to permit an idea to have
power in our lives or reject it. The heart controls
our will.

To learn how to meditate, most people need to set
aside specific times to calm their minds so they can
become aware of the thinking/feeling self deep
inside. Because people experience God's presence
differently, it may take you some time to discover
what sort of questions or images help you focus on
your heart.

The following are some tips that may help you.
Pausing to meditate in the morning and the
evening is the Biblical norm (Psalm 1:2). It is a good
idea to choose a regular time each day. Most people
find the morning is best. In the evening, after the
members of your household have gone to their
rooms, can be good also. Many people meditate sitting up. Others kneel or stand. Some people go to a

nearby church during their lunch hour. Most people find that if they lie down and then disengage from the busyness of their lives, they fall asleep.

Choose a quiet place. I have a couch I really like in a room that is quiet and away from the kitchen. Have a Bible handy, maybe two or three versions. Keep paper or a notebook and a pen nearby. I have a binder in which I keep my God sightings on the form in Appendix A. I also have a notebook for more extensive thoughts.

Is there some object that reminds you of God? My grandfather's Bible reminds me that what I am doing is ageless. Some people have a picture of Jesus, or a copy of the sculpture "Praying Hands" or the "Pieta." Some people find music helpful. Other people like to look out a window. One friend of mine meditates with his dog's head in his lap.

The problem is not that meditation is hard. It is perfectly natural. The problem is that most people are terribly distracted. This preparation helps you avoid needless disruptions so you can remain connected to your heart. An awareness of God's living presence is in your hearts or inner self. Jumping up to get something kills the moment. It takes time to resettle. Once you learn how to manage the distraction of your life and listen for the conversation of your heart, you will be able to meditate anywhere and at any time.

If you are in a group and first read these suggestions at your meeting place, reread them when you get to the place you will use during the week. Prepare your space to be convenient and comfortable,

then complete the preparations outlined in the first
set of direction for leaders in each chapter.

Preparing to Meditate

As you use this book in the week ahead, read
everything in regular type normally. Read italicized
portions calmly and slowly because that is relaxing.
Do not rush. Anything in italics is to be read one
thought at a time and repeated silently. Doing this
helps many people direct the words to their hearts.
When leading yourself through these exercises, you
may find reading them out loud then repeating
them silently helps you hear the conversation of
your heart. Others hear this deeper conversation by
reading silently once. Experiment and discover
what works for you.

When you are asked to listen, you are being asked to
listen for the conversation of your heart. Listen without conscious effort or control. Many people say that
they feel as though the conversation comes up from
within or below their normal train of thought.

People differ on how their hearts converse. Though
it is common to use words, some people think on
this deeper level in images. Some people feel or intuit. You will quickly discover your style. The conversation of your heart is what you hear just before
you fall asleep or when you daydream.

Put both feet on the floor. It is probably best not
to cross your legs. Crossing your legs can create
pressure points and over time even distracting
pain. Place your hands palms up on your forelegs.

Say,

*A note to leaders:
Since these
exercises are built
on prayers, it is
natural for people
to close their eyes.
Ask them to open
them when done
so you know when
to continue.*

Become aware of your breathing. Breathe in the air that sustains life. As you breathe out, relax. Starting at the top of your head, move the center of your awareness down your body. Relax each muscle group. Be aware of the area around your ears and relax any unnecessary tension. Move to your eyes, your jaw, your neck and your shoulders. Relax unnecessary tension. Move to your arms, hands. Now move to your back, your abdomen, your hips, your legs, your ankles, your feet and your toes.

Scripture

Say,

From the time your mother first told you to hurry up and take your bath, people have been training you to be quick. Too much mental agitation, however, blocks meditation. This exercise is based on Psalm 23. It is training of how to create a quiet center in the midst of your soul. There are two other exercises later on that help you do the same thing. As you work through the next seven weeks, if you cannot focus, return to this exercise and dwell on it. If you get nothing else from this book, getting this can be a tremendous help to you.

Repeat each thought quietly to yourself using the voice you hear when you are falling asleep or daydreaming. Be aware of your response.

Pray. Remember to pause after each thought.

"Come Holy Spirit and enter my heart. Quiet me so I become as relaxed as a small child in its mother's lap. In Christ's name. Amen."

As you read this, repeat each phrase to yourself and be aware of any response from within:

The Lord is my shepherd, I shall not want.
He makes me lie down in green pastures;
he leads me beside still waters;
he restores my soul.
He leads me in the right paths for his name's sake.
Even though I walk through the darkest valley,
I fear no evil; for you are with me;
your rod and your staff - they comfort me.
You prepare a table before me in the presence
of my enemies;
you anoint my head with oil; my cup overflows.
Surely goodness and mercy shall follow me
in all the days of my life,
and I shall dwell in the house of the Lord
my whole life long. (Psalm 23 NRSV)

In your mind, return to the words "he leads me beside still waters." Repeat these words silently each time you exhale. Repeat four or five times.

Read the following slowly and quietly. Pause after each image, allowing time to respond to the images. You may find it helpful to repeat each thought quietly once you have read it. Listen from within yourself. If you think in images, allow a picture to form in your mind's eye. Some of you will neither hear a conversation nor see images but will be aware of God's presence anyhow. People differ.

"You are walking along a path in the woods beyond a pleasant field. A brook is next to the path. Damp cool air meets your nostrils. You breathe in the freshness. You can smell the damp, pleasant aromas of the woods. What does your stream look like or sound like? Do you put your foot in it? Do you sit on a stone with Jesus sitting

Quietly say the words, "He leads me beside still waters" four times. Then ask the group to open the book to page 7 and do the exercise that begins with "Read the following…"

7

next to you? What is the sound you hear? What do you feel? What do you know? Do you see nothing in your mind but feel yourself relax anyhow at the thoughts? It makes no difference how you recall the calmness of a babbling brook. Just relax and dwell by gently flowing, quiet waters."

Wait three minutes. Say,

Has your mind relaxed a bit? If so, ask yourself, "Have I just experienced God's love refreshing my spirit?"

If so, thank God for the gift.

The First Cycle of Exercises:
Lord Do You Love Me?

"Give me a God-listening heart" (1 Kings 3:9 TM).

Exercise One: Listening to Our Hearts for Our Experience of God's Love

Say,

"Dear Lord, when have I known that you are love? Help me recall where I was. Who I was with? What was going on, Lord, and why I was struck by your love?"

Pause.

"Lord, let me see a time that your love impressed me."

Pause.

"Jesus, what was going on when your love got my attention?"

When most people have opened their eyes, say,

Using the God Sightings form, write down a few words that will help you to recall your experience of the love of God. Return thanks to God for being with you.

Exercise Two: Listening for a Time
When God Has Loved Me Recently

Say,

Having gotten in touch with the fact that you can
find God's loving presence in your life, limit the
timeframe to a week to ten days. Over time you
will become better at disengaging from the clutter
of your life. It then becomes easier to sense the
presence of the God who loves you. Repeat this
prayer with the deepest part of yourself:

Pray,

*"Lord, what was happening when I knew you were
around recently?"*

Pause.

"You call me friend. Show yourself to me."

Pause.

*"I know that you are love. Help me. When have you been
present, Jesus?"*

Pause.
Say,

Make notes using the form called God Sightings
(Appendix A) and thank God for loving you.

Exercise Three: Preparing to Love Another
with Christ's Love

*After they make
their notes say,*

The first two exercises are designed to help you relate
the statement in 1 John 4:8, "God is love," to your
personal experience of God. The next exercise helps
you to base your actions on Jesus' new command to
love others with the love you meet in Christ (John
13:34). If you have an active imagination, this
exercise may be especially effective for you. Also, if
you are likely to daydream, you will do better with
meditation if you engage your imagination in the
process. Doing that helps you to remain focused.

Pick about three people each time you meditate this week. Ask God to help you recall when and how you loved them. I encourage you to start with the people you are most familiar with: those you live with, those you work with and those whom you will see because they are a part of your church or social group.

Relax. Give yourself time between each sentence to respond.

Pray,

"Let us pray. Lord, whom would you have me think about today? Let me be aware of that person. Help me imagine them as clearly as I can. I notice the expression of their face, the way their hair is combed. Lord, help me see what they are wearing, whether they have shaved, their posture. Name their name and ask them to tell you

Pause.   *what they wish from you today."*

Pause.   *"Lord, whom do you want me to be especially aware of?"*

Pause.   *"Lord, whom would you have me touch with your love?"*

Make a note of any response on an index card or scrap of paper. If it seems appropriate and you are able, give them the gift they ask for. Date the note and call it something like Memo from God or Ministry List. Keep it at hand and, after you have done what you sensed you could do for Christ, mark it complete and date when you did it. Keep the notes for use during Week Five.

This completes the first cycle of three exercises. A meditation cycle is two or more related exercises that make up a whole. When you get to the last one, start over again. Each day, begin with the Preparation, go to the Scripture, and then pick up where you left off with the cycle. If it takes two days or three days to complete the cycle, fine. Don't rush to complete the set. Hurry is the enemy of meditation, and agenda anxiety often drives busyness.

Each day this week, begin where you left off the day before and use this cycle for about 15 minutes. Remember to take notes on the form provided. Also, return thanks to God for being present in love to you. During four or five of the next seven days, take time, perhaps in the evening, to read one of the offerings in Going Deeper. There are five of them that relate to this session. You may discover that it takes you more than one day to complete one. Take the time you need so that you do not rush through them.

If you draw a complete blank on Exercise One, jump down to Exercise Three. It is common to have no response to one or more exercises any particular day. Because this is a cycle of exercises, you will return to any exercise you draw a blank on.

Also, only be concerned about repeating the God-listening prayers if your mind wanders off. Otherwise, relax and let the Spirit take you where it will. *If you are a member of a group, remember to keep your notes in an orderly fashion and take them to the next meeting.*

Close with prayer.

Going Deeper

This week you have five things to ponder and make notes on. You will probably want a separate notebook to record your thoughts in. The God Sightings form does not provide adequate space. If you are part of a group, bring your notes, memos and God Sightings to the next meeting.

Day One: The Holy Spirit

The work of the Holy Spirit is to help us find traces of God's love when we listen to our experience. What I will say about the Spirit is limited by the focus of this book. If you want to know more, I recommend starting with Catherine Marshall's book *The Helper*.[2]

The Holy Spirit moves God's love from being an idea to being a living presence. This happens in a variety of ways. One spectacular way of encountering God's love is through a vision. As a priest Isaiah worshipped in the temple often. He had prayed the Psalms regularly. He was entirely familiar with passages like God sits "enthroned between the cherubim" (Psalm 80:1) and "the earth is the Lord's and the fullness thereof" (Psalm 24:1 KJV). One day, the Holy Spirit touched Isaiah. He was filled with a vision:

> *In the year that King Uzziah died, I saw the Lord seated on a throne, high and exalted, and the train of his robe filled the temple. Above him were seraphs, each with six wings: With two wings they covered their faces, with two they covered their feet, and with two they were flying. And they were calling to one another:*
> *"Holy, holy, holy is the LORD Almighty;*
> *the whole earth is full of his glory."*
> *At the sound of their voices the doorposts and thresholds shook and the temple was filled with smoke.* (Isaiah 6:1-4).

---

2 Catherine Marshall, *The Helper* (Waco, Texas: Word Books, 1979).

For eons people have used their imagination to give their thoughts a focus. In all likelihood Isaiah imagined what it would be like to see God often. This time Isaiah ceased simply thinking about God. God became as real to Isaiah as the floor he was standing on.

The Spirit works in other ways as well. People who do not have visions still know God loves them just as surely as Isaiah did. John Wesley felt his heart "strangely warmed" while hearing a sermon on Luther's commentary on Romans. Other people hear God's presence rather than see it. Joan of Arc is a famous example. Do not be concerned about the pathway by which you personally become aware of God's loving presence. All of them are available to the Spirit and all of them result in the same sort of change in people.

The Holy Spirit also makes people aware of things that they just cannot know by ordinary means. Have you ever called a friend or family member you were suddenly thinking about for no reason, only to discover that they have had something important happen? Perhaps they just came home from an operation or a child got engaged. When our calls are just so perfectly timed, it is just more sensible to thank the God who loves us both than to say, "Wow, what a coincidence!"

Through all these ways and more the Holy Spirit makes God's presence known to us. If you are not aware of the Spirit's activity in your life, all of this will sound strange. Once you become aware of that presence, all of this will make perfect sense. Listening to others' experience is the best way I know to discover the movement of the Spirit whispering about God's love.

For Further Thought or Discussion:
- Whom do you know who talks about being touched by the Holy Spirit? What sort of difference does the Spirit make in their lives?
- Have you had the experience of receiving an insight that felt like a gift? If so, what was it?
- When do you feel God as a living presence?

Journal and Share.

Day Two: Discernment and God's Love

God is love and those who abide in love know God (1 John 4:16). Yet, far
more than God resides between our ears. John writes that we must test
the spirits when we meditate because not everything we hear represents
God (1 John 4:1). Paul reminds us that one of the great benefits of turning our lives over to God is an increased ability to discern God's Spirit
(Romans 12:2).

Each cycle of exercises begins with a variation on the simple question
"Lord, do you love me?" Reflecting on the answers we hear tells us a
great deal about ourselves. It is also an excellent place to begin to learn
discernment.

The truth is that God is love. When we turn to our internal dialogue, the
voice we hear that affirms that God is love speaks the truth. That voice
is true even if it is a living memory of someone we lived with as a child.
It is true whether we are feeling cheerful or stressed or unhappy. Our
emotional state does not determine God's attitude toward us. The truth
of the "yes" we hear when we ask, "Lord, do you love me?" depends
solely on God.

Other answers we hear, and we all hear them, represent a false
understanding even though they may feel entirely natural to us and be
rooted deeply in our experience. A friend of mine growing up was told
regularly by his father that he was no good. After I became a minister,
he asked me one day if he could pray to "Our Mother" since "Our
Father" always brought back terribly negative thoughts. I suggested he
pray to Jesus Christ to avoid the problem. I pointed out to him that he
understood more clearly than most what falsehood in his heart he had
to learn to push aside and disregard if he wanted to grow to be more
like Christ. No matter how natural his negative thoughts were to him,
they were all denials of the good news that, in love, God values us.

When I ask God, "Lord, do you love me?" I usually hear, "Yes." As I
consider the spirit behind these words, that spirit is an affirming spirit.

Even if I am remembering something my mother or my brother said to me once, the spirit behind the words reflects God's nature.

When I ask, "Lord, do you love me?" I occasionally hear quite a different message. Sometimes I hear a voice that answers "Of course I do." Those words express a different spirit to me. Those words sound like someone who is impatient with the question and somewhat offended. If I remember correctly, my mother was generally impatient with me asking her for reassurance.

As important as words are, we also have to look beyond the words to the spirit they express. For you, the phrase, "Of course I do," may express a father's or a mother's open-armed reassurance that you are loved. In that case, the spirit expressed by those words would reflect the truth about God to you as surely as they do not to me. This is why each one of us has to learn how to discern the spirits within our own soul. Though the principles are straightforward, their applications are unique to each person.

Once we allow ourselves to hear what is going on around us, the next step is to learn to listen to others as God listens to them. God listens for the spirit behind the words:

The lamp of the LORD searches the spirit of a man; it searches out his inmost being (Prov. 20:27).

When we discern the spirit behind the words, we ponder both our lives and our neighbors' lives from a different perspective. As God does with us, we look to another's heart. Like God, we look through the eyes of love. Though we cannot see as clearly as God sees, we see much more than when we are rushing though life.

For Further Thought or Discussion:
- Think of someone who has trouble trusting others. How does their distrust affect their judgment?
- Think of someone who trusts others. How does their basic trust affect their judgment?

15

- What do you think of the statement "If we trust God, we will probably make better decisions because we allow ourselves to hear what other people really mean when they talk."?

Journal and Share.

Day Three: Discernment and Potential Acts of Ministry

Exercise Three focuses on our ministry to others. If we are going to love them properly, we need to look at the spirit behind the suggestion before acting on it (John 4:1). Does the spirit express the sort of love we find in Jesus Christ? Here are two examples:

Example One: This morning I held up Dick in my prayers. Dick is a client who recently had a medical procedure. He does not think of himself as a Christian, but he is interested in "spiritual stuff." Like many, he watches professing Christians to see if our lives are consistent with our beliefs. As I prayed for him, I sensed that God was encouraging me to call. I felt a small tug at my heart, a sort of whispered "Just do it" and Jesus specifically said that we should pay attention to the sick (Mt. 25:36). The spirit behind the thought was one of genuine concern, so a picked up the phone and called.

Example Two: I recently felt an urge to call a colleague whom I usually avoid. I had had a sales success with a type of business that I know she was having trouble selling. The thought on the surface looked caring. I was going to help her by sharing my technique for success.

I asked God to show me the spirit behind the words and waited. I soon realized that I really wanted to tell her how much better at this I was than she was. The last time we were together, she was basically telling everyone, "I am better at this than you, would you not agree?" I am not alone in finding her obnoxious. I cannot remember, though, where Jesus says, "Truly, truly I say to you, if you find them obnoxious, rub their nose in your success every opportunity you have." I decided to not call

16

her. I handed my resentment over to God's care this morning. I will probably have to give it back to God again soon because I will be seeing her tomorrow.

For Further Thought or Discussion:
- Ask God to help you recall when you have seen someone say they were caring for another but it was clear to you and others that they we doing something hurtful.
- How do you tell the difference between caring and being nasty-nice in others?
- How do you tell the difference in your life?

Journal and Share.

Day Four: Meditation Does Not Just Sit on the Couch

As I was writing this chapter on love, I used each of the exercises and made notes. Looking for God's love and how we have honored Christ's new command can be embarrassing, but even that is good.

I listened in my heart after asking God to show me whom I had loved in Christ's name during the last day. I remembered that I fixed dinner for my wife. That was a good finish, but let me tell you about the start.

We live in the frozen North. My wife went downhill skiing today. Afterwards, she worked for about a half-hour, then went to the doctor's. A contact lens got stuck in her eye, and it shredded when she pulled it out. Maybe a piece was still in there and would cause a problem. The doctor determined that she had gotten it all. So she returned home and was standing in the kitchen bleaching the kitchen trashcan when I came home.

You know you are in love when your wife is bleaching the trashcan and still looks good after 37 years. She sat down, and I asked her about her day. I discovered it was mostly monkey business and sitting in the doctor's office.

I had been busy, busy, busy and had made a couple of sales. I was a happy camper but ready for dinner. I was casting about for an argument to motivate her to fix dinner when she was done with the trashcan. "This should be easy," I thought, "I worked and made money. She played and got tired. I deserve dinner."

Years of meditation have taught me that the words "I deserve" never come from God and always tend towards unhappiness. The spirit behind the words is one of phony entitlement at the expense of others. I paused in my thoughts in order to imagine that Jesus was sitting next to my wife and would say to me something more useful than what I was saying to myself.

I got up and fixed her dinner. She liked that a lot. That was a small gift. It was mostly microwaving. Thirty-seven years of exchanging small gifts and the occasional large one has done wonders for our relationship. We started out as two prickly, competitive, self-absorbed, overgrown children. We still can be all those things. Through one experience at a time we have both drawn closer to God. As we come closer to God, we come closer to each other. Because God is love, the presence of God creates community.

For Further Thought or Discussion:
- Do you ever try to look nice while manipulating others?
- What is a small gift in your life that had a big effect?

Journal and Share.

Day Five: The Power of Meditation

A lifetime of familiarity with meditation and the Scriptures is powerful. Opening our hearts to God's love this way can deeply affect how we experience even the most difficult moments of our lives. One afternoon as I was sitting in his room, my father lay in a hospital bed dying of cancer. He whispered to himself, "Eloi, Eloi, lama sabachthani" the first words of Psalm 22 in Hebrew. These words are quoted in the Gospels. Like his Lord and also King David before him, my father used this psalm to pour out his heart in sorrow and in hope. Unlike Jesus and David, my father had not been betrayed by either family or friends. He was, however, allergic to morphine and could not take the painkillers most people take in his condition.

He was in intense pain that day and still covered in hives from his allergic reaction to morphine. He asked me to scratch his back. Touching his skin was one of the most difficult things I ever did. He was hot, dry and covered with lumps.

My father was nearly overwhelmed by all he was suffering. He whispered the words Jesus and David had used in their pain. I encourage you to read the entire psalm. It ends with David remembering other times that he had felt hopeless only to experience that God was with him and he was lifted up and ultimately walked into Jerusalem as a part of a victory celebration. My father was more than ready for death. He was thinking of victory also, joining the saints before the throne of God in heaven. I caught snatches of the psalm as he continued to recite it.

He then whispered the first words of the hymn, "For All the Saints." He continued in silence, then relaxed visibly and found a short time of peace. He had withdrawn into a place within his soul that he had cultivated for years. After a while the pain pulled him out of his place of rest. He managed a faint smile and his eyes spoke of a reality beyond the moment.

It broke my heart to see my father this way. It filled my heart to see him escape his current condition into the reality of God's presence and find peace and relief, if only for a short time. He was grateful. Who was I to consider what he valued a small gift? I went to see him intending to give him any sort of good gift I could. Instead, I left having received a gift. Though my father thought that his situation was totally ridiculous, a lifetime of meditation was one of the few resources left to him to find peace. In truth, God is love.

19

For Further Thought or Discussion:
- Whom do you know who has a deep, strong relationship with God? What sorts of pain does that relationship help them bear?
- At times we all deal with difficult things in our lives. What difference does it make to know that God is with you (Psalm 23:4-5) rather than your being alone in your situation?

Journal and Share.

You will quickly discover that your answers to the Going Deeper questions will take up more space than the God Sightings form provides. Most people use a separate notebook for writing out their thoughts. Review your God Sightings and any memos on ministry once a week. Share your insights with a friend. *If you belong to a group, take your notes with you.*

Week Two:
Lord, Do You Understand Me?

Before you start, get your God Sightings and Memos together. Have blank forms. Have something to write with.

In the quiet between each thought, repeat the thought to yourself silently. Then be still and listen for the presence of the God who understands you. You are his beloved creation. Let us pray:

"Listening Lord, you understand us even before we have the words to speak. You are able to judge our hearts' intention even when we are confused. We open our hearts to you. We invite the Spirit to enter. Give us Solomon's gift, a God-listening heart, so we might understand the difference between what is from Christ and what cannot be. Grant us wisdom as we love those around us. In Christ's name. Amen."

You are understood. You were created intentionally by a loving God. Therefore, you are understood even when others do not understand you and even when you feel alone. Being understood is a gift you were offered at birth from God. This week you will learn to look for love as understanding and to consider how you can minister to others through un-

Leaders, have extra blank forms available.

Say,

As you lead in prayer, pause after each thought.

Pause.

derstanding. Believing that no one understands them, many people keep busy to avoid their sense of being alone. You do not have to be one of them. You are understood by and in fellowship with God.

You will learn a new way to journal and to use your daily experiences to draw closer to God and to your neighbor. The exercises focus on love as understanding. Understanding comes first because people cannot enter into community with others unless they understand them and believe that they can be understood.

You will also learn two other practices of the spiritual life: reviewing recent God sightings and meditating on the Scriptures.

Invitation to Journaling

Review the following. If you are with others, take turns reading.

Christian meditation provides a way to read both the Scriptures and the events of our lives with our hearts. Most of us are then tempted to rush back into the routine of our daily lives. Journaling encourages us to take the time to search for the words to express our insights. Having written them down, we are much more likely to remember them. Sharing our insights with one or more people is a powerful encouragement to Christian growth and ministry. The process of journaling and sharing leads to wisdom. Wisdom can be defined as practical knowledge about how to influence people and manage situations. Remember Solomon's request, "Give me a God-listening heart" (1 Kings 3:9 TM). Journaling helps us to develop such a heart.

You are already journaling when you use the God Sightings form. The form focuses our attention on where we sense God's presence in our daily lives. This week I encourage you to get a notebook of some sort and write down your thoughts about the Scripture passages and your responses to the questions that follow each Going Deeper story. In time your notebook will become a powerful tool by which you integrate your faith with your experience. Once a week read the entire week's entries. Share your insights with another. You will be amazed.

Preparing to Meditate

Divide the group into pairs. Say,

Prepare yourself to meditate by taking your center of awareness down from the top of your head to your toes, relaxing each major muscle group as you do. Begin by praying this prayer within the quiet of your own heart. Pause after each phrase so that you can repeat the prayer silently to yourself.

"Loving God, by your spirit be present to me as I search my experience for your presence. I open my heart to you. In Christ's name. Amen."

Reread six or so God Sightings notes from last week. In your mind's eye relive one of those moments as fully as you can. Where were you? Whom were you with? What was going on? Why would you say that God was there? Then thank God for each moment.

Wait two minutes.

Having reviewed your experience with God's love, one from each pair share with your partner a moment you knew God loved you last week.

23

Wait two minutes.	
	Thank you. Let's switch and the other one share.
Wait two minutes.	

Scripture

Read,	*O LORD, you have searched me* *and you know me.* *You know when I sit and when I rise;* *You perceive my thoughts from afar…* *Before the word is on my tongue* *you know it completely, O LORD* (Psalm 139:1-2,4).
Pray, *Pause.*	"Lord, what do you want me to hear?"
	Does some word or phrase stand out? If so, ask God to show you what he wants you to understand. If you are drawing a blank, pray the following with me and listen.
Pause.	
	"Lord, when did I know you understood me like the author of the psalm?"
Pause.	
	"Lord, when did I feel understood?"
	If you sense no response from the first two prayers, pray,
Pause.	
	"Lord above, show me what you want me to see."
	Return thanks and make your notes on the God Sighting form. Keep your notes brief. God will help you remember the rest if it is really important.
Wait three minutes.	

We will now focus on God's recent gifts of under-standing. If you are aware of other ways God has loved you, fine. Make a note of them as well and thank God for the gift.

Say,

The Second Cycle of Exercises: Understanding

"Give me a God-listening heart" (1 Kings 3:9 TM).

Exercise One: Listening for the Truth in Our Lives

Relax, take a deep breath and let it out. Breathe in normally. As you exhale, pray the God-listening prayer:

Say,

Pause.

"Lord, do you understand me?" Listen.

Pause.

If your mind is wandering, try a different way. Pray,

"Lord, do you know what I need?" Listen.

Pause.

"Lord, do you hear me when I call?" Listen.

Pause.

Listen for the "Yes," however you experience it. Be aware that you may hear, see, feel, or sense other answers. That is common. Since God is a God who loves through understanding, any voice you are aware of that does not say, "Yes," speaks for itself and not for God.

Make a note in your notebook of any negative or qualified answers to the question "Lord, do you love me?" These answers are not biblical. They are the foundation of thoughts and behaviors that deny what Christ taught. You will learn to recognize them in the midst of everyday decision-making and pass by them without acting on them. When you review your notebook at the end of the week, I encourage you to spend some time exploring the attitudes that express your non-Christ-like beliefs and the types of actions they encourage. Just ask God what he wants you to understand about the negative answers you carry around between your ears.

Allow time for notes.

Exercise Two: Listening to Our Experience for the Gifts We Receive

Say,

After repeating each thought silently to yourself, listen without conscious effort to control your thoughts. Just be aware of the words, phrases, feelings or impressions that come to you.

Pray, pausing after each thought. Pause.

"Lord, show me where I was when you understood me in the last several days."

Pause.

"Lord, have I felt your understanding recently?" Listen.

"Lord, show me that you know who I am and what I need." Listen.

Pause.

If your mind is racing and you need to slow down, ignore the rest of the exercises. Rather, turn to the exercise based on Psalm 23 at the bottom of page 7. After using it, return to the first prayer, "Lord, do you understand me?"

If your mind is calm and you simply did not connect with the exercise, do not worry about it. Perhaps you will when you return to it later in the week.

Exercise Three: Recalling the Gifts We Give

Relax, take a deep breath, then let it out. Breathe in normally. When I ask you to listen, be still and without effort allow yourself to be aware of the dialogue of your heart.

Say,

"Where was I when I understood another, Lord?" Listen.

Pray,

Pause.

"Lord, did I love another with understanding yesterday? Show me." Listen.

Pause.

"Lord, who have I encouraged by being understanding?" Listen.

Give yourself a few minutes to write down one or two of your experiences. Thank God for the opportunities you have had to love others with the love we meet in Jesus Christ.

Exercise Four: Listening for God's Guidance for Our Ministry to Others

Relax and settle. If you need to, begin again at the top of your head and move your center of awareness down, relaxing any tension you may have accumulated.

Pause, then say,

Pause.

27

Pause.

"Lord, is there anyone I know who needs understanding?" Listen.

"Lord, show me people who need me to understand them." Listen.

Pause.

"Lord, whom do I know who hungers for understanding?" Listen.

Pause.

On an index card, make notes of any acts of love you feel God may want you to do and date it. Other types of loving acts are likely to come to you. Great! Make notes of them as well. Remember to make ministry notes each day, date them and keep them. When you have done it, date it again and make a note about the result. Thank God for the opportunities you have had to love others with the love we meet in Jesus Christ (John 13:34).

Wait two minutes. Say,

This completes the cycle for this week. Remember that it is neither necessary nor even desirable to try to complete each exercise every day. You already know how to rush so practice giving yourselves time to dwell in the flow of thoughts, feelings and impressions when it happens. Take the time to understand what you are experiencing. You can always begin where you left off the next day. To restart, go to the Preparing to Meditate section (page 23) and follow it until you get to the exercises. Start with the exercise you did not finish the day before.

Narrowing your prayer focus to just one aspect of God's love may help you to develop concrete ways to love others with the love you meet in Jesus Christ. Below are four additional readings. Each day I encourage you to pick one reading and spend 15 to 20 minutes with it. Many people prefer the evening for doing this. If you do not get finished with a reading, pick it up the next day.

Before starting the next cycle of exercises, review your notes and take time to ask God to show you what he wants you to understand. If part of a group, bring all of your notes to the next meeting. Read over all of them weekly.

Close with a prayer of thanksgiving for quiet time and for God's presence.

Going Deeper

This week you have four items to consider. If you have the time, pick up any you missed last week or repeat one that spoke to you. Remember, meditation is about learning the art of mentally chewing on an experience until you see the hand of God at work in your life and the lives of others. Do not rush and do not worry if you draw a blank on a question or exercise.

Day One: Reflections on the Scripture

God understands us. The conversation of our heart that affirms this truth is correct. Voices within our hearts that contradict this truth do not speak for God. It may be true that people who are important to us do not understand us, but it is never true that we are not understood. God has searched us and knows us.

You may know this is true already. You may have to search for this experience. Whatever the case, the truth of the statement "God understands us" does not depend on how you feel or what you think. It depends on God. God is a God who understands.

Look again at your responses that affirm something other than the truth that God loves you. For some of us, important people in our lives were preoccupied, perhaps with themselves and their needs or perhaps with a career. Some of us were raised in households with an addicted family member. Others lived with people who desired to be perfect. Whatever your story, many people are convinced that they are not and cannot be understood. A belief that we are not understood gives rise to a whole set of thoughts, reactions and patterns of behavior that lead us to inappropriate and even hurtful responses to others.

As you become aware that these patterns are, on a practical level, a denial of the gospel, you will also become aware of your freedom to hand them over to God in order to experience healing, release and new life.

Discernment (1 John 4:1) is the process of becoming aware of the difference between which patterns of thought express the truth and which ones are false. Discernment is rooted in Scripture and aided by the living presence of the Holy Spirit. These may just sound like empty phrases to you now. Allow yourself to see the difference, then pray for freedom. You can hand the junk over to God and be amazed at the results.

As you become more aware of the difference in how false and true patterns of thought feel and sound, you also become better at sensing what future possibilities may come from God and which possibilities are contrary to God's nature.

For Further Thought or Discussion:
- Why is it important to realize that the truth about our relationship with God depends on God and not on our opinions about God or how we feel?
- Why is it not important who first taught us that we are understood but vitally important to remember that we are understood no matter what is going on in our lives?

Journal and Share.

Day Two: God's Love is Lavish

God understands what we need and puts the right people into our lives. Today my wife came down the stairs and asked, "Want to go on a walk?"

"With you?" I asked.

As I write this, winter is settling in. It snowed recently. The creeks are still running but beginning to freeze. Feet crunching in the snow, we walked to a local waterfall. We stood still. All around us was blue sky, white clouds, rushing water, wonderful ice formations stretching thirty feet down the face of the waterfall. A couple we know walked up and we met their new dog, a wonderful animal. We started crunching back down the trail to home. I realized that I had a bounce in my step.

Exercise is good for us, of course. Beautiful scenery on a blue-sky day lifts the soul. Neighbors and a nice dog are certainly positive things. Nonetheless, I have walked the path, seen the waterfall and talked to neighbors many times. Today, however, it was as though God knew exactly what I needed and provided it through my wife and others. My heart touched a loving presence just beyond comprehension, yet close. God has known me and searched me and gifted me today in a remarkable way. And that is just today.

God knows who we are. At times we simply know that is true. The web of circumstance of our lives whispers of a realm both beyond and very near, the realm of the God who once knelt by the river, formed us from the clay and breathed us full of God-breath (Gen. 2:7). If we are truly made in the image of God and designed for fellowship, we would expect to have such moments.

For Further Thought or Discussion
- When have you discovered that God has provided exactly what you needed through others and the circumstances of your life?

Journal and Share.

Day Three: God Understands that Returning Thanks Changes Us

God understands how to transform our lives. Given my personal history, it is always a miracle to me when I can enjoy even something as simple as a walk in the woods. I spent years worrying about all sorts of things. Then one day I was reading the story of Gabriel telling Mary she was going to give birth to Jesus, the Christ. These words caught my attention: "Do not be afraid" (Luke 1:30).

When the angels appeared to the shepherds, they also said, "Do not be afraid" (Luke 2:10). It dawned on me. God said the same thing over and over again. "Do not be afraid." Fear does not come from God. This was one of those moments of fresh insight, a new beginning. I was touched all the way to the center of my heart by a truth I had heard for years. Since God is love, there is no place for fear of judgment or anxiety in our walk with God (1 John 4:18, Mt. 6:25-34).

Somehow the following verse really stuck in my heart. Paul said,

> *Finally, brothers, whatever is true, whatever is noble, whatever is right, whatever is pure, whatever is lovely, whatever is admirable—if anything is excellent or praiseworthy—think about such things. Whatever you have learned or received or heard from me, or seen in me—put it into practice. And the God of peace will be with you* (Phil. 4:8-9).

I never had trouble seeing what might cause pain or loss. Learning to let the heart dwell on the good, the noble and the beautiful allows me to see the rest of life. God has enabled me to see the wonder and be grateful. If you have not discovered it already, dwelling on the gifts will draw you close to the heart of God as well. Truly, God understands how to transform our lives by addressing our needs.

For Further Thought or Discussion:
- Why does thanking God affect how we think about our lives?
- What is the difference between being grateful for what is right and pretending that bad things don't exist?
- Why do many people admire optimists but wonder if people who are always positive understand the real world?

Journal and Share.

Day Four: Remembered from Childhood: When I Met Joseph in My Mother

In difficult times God understands what stories we need in order to make sense of our lives. In August of 1949 my father was the British Consul General of Canton, China. The Communists were dashing towards the south of China. Western Nations were evacuating their citizens from Canton. Because my mother was already six and a half months pregnant when the decision to evacuate was made, we were among the last to leave.

As we waited for my sister Elsie to be born and get large enough to fly, the city was surrounded. We went to sleep at night with the flash of howitzers on the horizon and the rumble of heavy guns.

The entire foreign community was required to live on Shamian Island, a 14-acre European enclave in the Pearl River. The river widens there and the area is called White Goose Pond. It was quickly filled with refugees living in little boats called sampans. Security was nearly non-existent. My mother put on a brave face, but when the furniture was shipped out and the servants fled, knocking around in a large, empty, silent house was terrifying. The silence in the house was so thick you could nearly touch it. It felt cold even in the heat of Canton, and I shivered.

On July 14, 1949 Elsie was born. Her birth brought us a step closer to leaving, but we were not permitted to fly yet. In those days, aircraft were not pressurized. At normal cruising altitudes newborns turned blue. Their lungs cannot adjust to the thin air. We waited another month, then made the short flight from Canton to Hong Kong. Every time the pilot got too high, Elsie turned blue and the stewardess would tell him he had to come down. The pilot was trying to avoid being hit by ground fire while the stewardess protected my baby sister. Together they got us there.

We spent a week in Hong Kong at the Peninsula Hotel. We then boarded a large seaplane called a PanAm Clipper and headed for my mother's native land, the United States. Elsie managed to remain relatively pink.

We flew to Louisville, Kentucky where my mother had been raised. As we got off the plane, several of my mother's friends met us. My mother had washed her face, put on a large hat with a feather in it and put on her best "everything is OK" face. Her friends drove us to what had been my grandmother's house. In time it became our home, but it felt strange at first.

Less than two months postpartum, my mother had left her husband in a war zone and taken her infant daughter and three older boys across the Pacific and two-thirds of the way across the United States to Kentucky. She was exhausted and not in very good shape.

At times it was all just too much for her. I would walk into a room to find her staring blankly into space or at a picture of her mother. It frightened me to see her that way. That is the thing I hated the most. It is like someone would come and steal my mother and leave a hollow shell. Then she would come to life again and perhaps be delightful, perhaps a whirlwind of activity, perhaps angry, but alive.

I came to discover how unstoppable my mother was. When she got knocked to the ground, she always got up. She was devoid of self-pity. At times she was tempted to feel sorry for herself, but she rejected that temptation. She taught us to ignore the whine inside and instead focus on what we could do. "Don't cry over spilt milk," she said. Her people had been dairy farmers in East Tennessee. She taught us, "If you cannot do anything about it, forget it and do what you can. Life is too precious to waste."

My mother's heritage was that of the steel magnolias of the South. She was raised on tales of gallantry and resourcefulness. Her heroine was Scarlett O'Hara from *Gone with the Wind*. Whenever she was overwhelmed, she looked at the house, tied a bandana around her hair and went to work. She was also raised listening to Bible stories. One of the characters that spoke to her was Joseph. A grand storyteller, she told me his story with excitement in her voice.

Joseph was the favored child. One day his jealous brothers sold him into slavery. In Egypt he made the best of each day. In time he became the manager of his master's household — a large, prosperous estate. Joseph was living well. His master's wife decided he was cute and tried to seduce him. Joseph refused her advances. In a fit of rage, she managed to get him arrested.

Imprisoned because of false accusations, Joseph made the best of his situation. Each day he did what he could. Recognizing the force of his character, the Master of the Guards presented him to the Pharaoh. Ultimately, Joseph saved many tens of thousands of people from starvation, including his own family. In the process Joseph made a huge sum of money for the Pharaoh. The Pharaoh made him treasurer of the realm and arranged for him to marry one of the Egyptian high priest's daughters. Joseph became the person God used to establish his people in Egypt.

Joseph did not waste his life nursing his resentments. He was a person after God's heart. The first time I met a person who lived like Joseph was on Glenmary Avenue, Louisville, Kentucky. Like Joseph my mother got up, dusted herself off and got back to the business of living. God understands the stories and the images we need to cultivate in order to handle the downside of our lives.

For Further Thought or Discussion:
- Whom do you know who is resilient? What is their gift to you?
- Perhaps you are the child of a parent who had a bitter outlook on life. Do you too think it normal to focus on hurt? If so, do you want to continue to allow a bitter spirit to rule in your heart? If the answer is no, I invite you to imagine yourself standing before the Christ. In your mind's eye, take the weight of bitterness from yourself and lay it at his feet. Pray words like, "Kind Lord, I have carried this bitterness too long. Forgive me. Take my anger,

disappointment, sorrow and bitterness. Show me what you would have me do with today. In your name. Amen." Pray this prayer each day for a week along with thanking God for what is right in your life, which is a part of these exercises. You have nothing to lose but a dead weight that is holding you in the past. Jesus Christ would set you free. Share your decision with a friend or pastor. Their encouragement and prayers can be of tremendous value to you at this time.

Journal and Share.

Review your God Sightings once a week and share your insights with a friend. *If you belong to a group, take your God Sightings journal with you to the next meeting.*

Week Three:
Lord, Do You Accept Me?

Leaders, have blank forms available.

Say,

Pause after each thought as you pray.

Pause.

Before you begin, have blank copies of the God Sightings forms and blank index cards and something to write with.

Repeat each thought to yourself giving yourself time to sense your response to the prayer. Let us pray,

"You who are both high and lifted up but also quietly present in the midst of the conversation of our hearts, help me become aware of your acceptance. You have made me a citizen of heaven and given me brothers and sisters. In Christ's name. Amen."

When people feel awkward or out of place, they often hide those feelings by keeping busy. There is a place for you. God accepts you. Acceptance, then is a part of loving others as Jesus has loved us (John 13:34).

This week we will look at another way to carry a quiet center into the activities of our lives. We will also explore a new way to use intercessory prayer. The Going Deeper section looks at intercessory prayer and at acceptance in various lights.

Carrying a Quiet Center into a Noisy Life

It is not possible to experience or to give acceptance on the fly. Cramming 30 hours of activity into 18 waking hours, many harried people exude a sense of jittery preoccupation. Christians who are deeply rooted in the Spirit may be busy, but they exude a sense of calm no matter what is around them. They live with Christ's peace (John 14:27).

Review the following. If you are with others, take turns reading.

Through meditation you can claim Christ's peace as your own. One way of doing this is to maintain a song in your heart. So many people respond so deeply to music that since the start Christians have filled their hearts with song and paused to return thanks:

> *Speak to one another with psalms, hymns and spiritual songs. Sing and make music in your heart to the Lord, always giving thanks to God the Father for everything, in the name of our Lord Jesus Christ* (Eph. 5:19-20).

To experiment with making music in your heart, pick a simple hymn that you know well and sing it to yourself. Practice it for two or three repetitions, then get up and do something routine like straightening up your tools or loading the dishwasher. When you are aware that you have stopped singing, start up again. About once an hour, take time to say the prayer, "Lord, what am I grateful for?" Take time to be aware and to give thanks for what is right in your life. If something spontaneously strikes you as right or beautiful or pleasant between these hourly prayers, thank God for that too. You never have to wait to be grateful.

Tomorrow, pick another hymn and do the same thing. If the hymn is not as familiar, practice it in the morning and evening for as long as it takes to make it completely familiar. Use it for two days if necessary. Most people quickly learn a half dozen psalms, hymns and spiritual songs they can sing as the day goes by.

Many people discover that they already sing but learn songs of greater value. Others say that in song they sense an even deeper intelligence at work in their hearts whom they naturally praise. A quiet center helps us see beyond ourselves as we seek to accept others as our Lord did when he lived among us. Listening to our everyday experience encourages wisdom. Wisdom and awareness are the twin platforms on which joy rests.

Preparing to Meditate

Have your group divide into pairs, then say,

Remember to repeat the God-listening prayers quietly to yourself.

Allow up to three minutes to complete this.

Prepare yourself to meditate. Put your feet on the floor and make yourself comfortable. Place your hands, palms up, in your lap. Become aware of your head. Starting at the top of your scalp, seek out areas in which you are carrying unnecessary tension and relax them. Let your breathing become steady and calm. Take your center of awareness down from the top of your head to your toes. Relax each major muscle group as you do. Let your mind wander without conscious control. When you are done, open your eyes.

"Lord of Life, light that shines in the darkness, help me see through the multitude of my experiences that fill up my brain. I want to see you in the midst of my life. In Christ's name. Amen."

Pray,

Pause.

Reread six or so God sightings from your journal. In your mind's eye, relive one or more of those moments. If you can, see the faces of the people involved in your mind's eye. If you can, replay what they said in your mind's ear. If you remember past events in a different way, that is fine. Substitute your style for this suggestion. Thank God for being present to you. When you are done, open your eyes.

Share at least one moment in which you experienced God's love last week.

After two minutes, switch partners.

Scripture

"But Ruth replied, 'Don't urge me to leave you or to turn back from you. Where you go I will go, and where you stay I will stay. Your people will be my people and your God my God'" (Ruth 1:16).

Read.

Pause.

"Lord, what would you have me hear in this story?"
Listen.

Pause.

"What do you hear? What words or images do you remember from the story?"

Pause.

"Lord, what would you have me see?"

Pause.

"Lord, what are you saying to me today?"

Pause.

41

Jot down your thoughts in your notebook. This week's focus is on acceptance. All of us need people to make a place for us in their hearts.

Allow up to three minutes for note taking.

The Third Cycle of Exercises: Accepting

"Give me a God-listening heart" (1 Kings 3:9 TM).

Exercise One: Listening to Our Hearts for Our Experience of God's Acceptance

Say,
Pause.

Sit back and relax. Breathe in normally.

"Lord, do you accept me?" Listen for the "yes" however it comes.

Pause.

"Lord, when did I feel that you included me in your circle of love?"

Pause.

If your mind is wandering, quietly sing something familiar like *"Joyful, Joyful We Adore Thee"* or *"Amazing Grace."*

Pause.

Make your notes on your God Sighting sheet, thanking God for each time you remember being included.

Pause three minutes. Say,

Look over your list. Are any answers not an unconditional "yes?" Note this in your notebook. That voice cannot speak for God. When you hear it, anything that it suggests is probably misguided. Practice moving beyond the counsels of this voice. Listen to those that speak the truth.

Do you sense no answer at all? It is common to initially hear no answer to our questions. It is a significant problem, however, for a Christian to attempt to love others with Christ's love without having an awareness of God's acceptance first. If you are unaware of God acceptance after a week, talk to a trusted friend or a pastor.

Exercise Two: Listening for the Gifts We Receive

"Lord, where was I when I experienced your acceptance?"

| | *Pray,* |

Pause.

"Lord, whom did you put into my life that delights in me?"

Pause.

"Lord, how have you shown me that I have a place in your heart?"

Pause.

After you have made your notes, take time to thank God for being in your life. As always you may be aware of other aspects of God's love. Jot those down also.

Exercise Three: Listening for the Gifts We Give

"Where was I and what was happening when I accepted another in your name?"

Pray,

Pause.

"Lord, whom did I include?"

Pause.

43

Pause.

"Show me how I have made a place for another yesterday."

When done, give yourself a few minutes to write down one or two examples of how you blessed another with the same sort of love you meet in God, especially love as acceptance. Thank God for the privilege of offering gifts of love to people who are a part of your life.

Exercise Four: Listening for God's Guidance for Our Ministry to Others

After three minutes, say,

Pray through your prayer list. If you do not keep a prayer list, you may want to refer to the form in Appendix D. For the moment, just go over the names of people you remember who need your prayers.

Pause three minutes. Say,

Do not be concerned if you have not completed your list. You can mark where you left off and return to it tomorrow. Relax. Take a deep breath then let it out. Breathe in normally. As you exhale, pray,

Pause.

"Whom would you have me accept today, Lord?"

Pause.

"Whom can I include today?"

Pause.

"Do I know someone who needs to feel at home?"

On an index card, write down the people and acts that God brought to your heart today. Date the card and carry it with you. These acts can serve as intentional acts of blessing that enrich your ministry to others and teach you new dimensions of love.

Thank God for each of these people and the possibilities of acceptance and love God just put in front of you. Review your ministry notes from previous days and mark the ones you have done and record the completion date. What are the results you are experiencing? Make a note of them as well.

Discernment (1 John 4:1)

Look over your list of possible acts and test the spirit of each one. Ask, "Did Jesus do similar things?" Question what the underlying feelings and motivations are. Are they worthy? Do they show love? Are they based on an expression of love that realizes that you are loved, understood and accepted, or are they based on some false premise?

Have the group turn to this page and take turns reading the following three paragraphs.

If you are unsure, look at your notebook and review the ways that you characteristically deny God's love. Are any of them involved with the action you are feeling unsure of? Is this a new area of service for you? The first several times we do something it is natural to be uneasy. If you are still unsure, share your thoughts with a friend. All of us need a Christian friend we can discuss things with. Another's eyes can help you see what you need to see in order to serve Christ.

If you are still unsure, just set the act aside and concentrate on the ones that you are sure express some aspect of God's love.

Pause.

45

If time permits, have the group share one or more of the Going Deeper offerings from last week. Close with prayer.

This concludes the third cycle of exercises, love as acceptance. *If you do not finish some days in the time allotted, do not rush. Tomorrow, start with prayer and a review of your God Sightings journal. Remember to return thanks to God, then resume where you left off. Use the Going Deeper section regularly. Remember, it is better to chew thoroughly on two of them than zip superficially through them all. Remember to review all current God Sightings and Memos at the end of the week. If you are in a group, keep your notes handy and take them to your next meeting.*

Going Deeper

This week you have a Bible reflection, two stories and two days worth of thoughts on intercessory prayer.

Day One: Reflections on the Scripture

The story of Ruth and Naomi is all about love as acceptance. Ruth said to Naomi, "Where you go I will go, and where you stay I will stay." This was probably a formal request to be adopted into Naomi's family. It was also a pledge to be loyal to Naomi and care for her. Ruth accepted Naomi as her own mother and pledged to treat her that way always. Older widows did not usually do well in ancient Israel. Ruth's offer was a beautiful, selfless thing to do.

This wonderful story is only four pages long. I encourage you to open your Bible and read all of it.

What Ruth did took courage. Even though Naomi could adopt her, she could not change the fact that Ruth was both a beautiful young childless widow and a Moabite. Being a beautiful young childless widow creates both opportunities and problems. Being a foreigner creates others.

In time, with Naomi's coaching, Ruth married a man named Boaz and had several children, one of whom was named Obed. He had a child named Jesse. Jesse had a child named David who became King of Israel.

Ruth was a good-hearted person, loyal to her friends and her mother-in-law. She was courageous, industrious and sensible and laughed easily. She trusted that God would be faithful and that in time her life would be put right side up again. God ignored her human label, "That Moabite Woman," and honored her heart. God accepts each one of us as we truly are and not as what we are according to human labels. God expects us to look beyond the label to see the person. If anyone is walking with the Lord, we must treat them as our sister or brother. That is what Christian acceptance is.

For Further Thought or Discussion:
- Whom do you know who can both be open about who they are and accepting of others as they actually are?
- What are the problems of seeing others as we hope they are and not as they actually are?
- Why do people see what they hope rather than what is there? How does faith in Jesus Christ help us to be wise as a fox though innocent at the same time?

Journal and Share.

Day Two: A Stranger in a Strange Land

As I remember my own struggle for acceptance, it was more than just having a mother who was sometimes with us and sometimes lost to us. America was a foreign country. On Shamian Island, Canton, I understood the rules. I had my routines and my friends. Life worked. Now I was in a place where even the toilets worked differently.

My mother did a lot of things right. When we arrived in America, she introduced me to a boy my own age, Brooke Turner. Since I had had an American friend in Canton, Brooke did not seem totally weird, just kind of weird. As an American he talked about things that I knew absolutely nothing about. He did things differently. He was amusing, though, and I needed badly to smile. He explained things and we enjoyed climbing trees and fences and exploring places we were told to stay out of.

Next to Brooke's house was a large vacant lot on which about 15 children age eight and younger played touch football. I immediately discovered that in spite of my knowing nothing about football, it had real possibilities. It involved lots of running about and shouting. We bumped into each other and piled on top of each other on the ground. There was a strange pointed ball called the pigskin, and the line of scrimmage or something moved all the time. There was offense and defense, first downs and all that other stuff. The game would clearly be great if I knew what I was doing.

On the way home after a confusing but better-than-average day in this place called America, I was passing by a house where an older woman was planting flowers. "Little boy," she called out, "are you Elsie Stewart's grandson?"

I stopped. "Yes, Madam, I am."

She laughed. "My but we are formal. Come over here. I knew your grandmother, a wonderful woman."

So we chatted a few minutes. Mrs. Courtney asked me how I was finding America. I answered, "Okay, I guess, but it would be better if I understood football." She smiled and said, "I have three grown sons. What do you want to know about football?"

Over the next several days as I walked back from Brooke's house I stopped by to help her with her flowers and learned about football. She taught me the rules and the names of the professional teams. She even taught me about the University of Kentucky Wildcats and that other team, Tennessee. After finding an old football, she showed me how to hold it and she chased me about the backyard. We laughed. Mrs. Courtney made a place in her heart and the routine of her day for a little stranger. Everything was not great, but it was getting better.

I believe that God was involved in this web of circumstances. I am not trying to convince you of anything. I am inviting you to use the tools of Christian faith to look at your life and see if it makes more sense with Christ.

It is absolutely typical of the God we meet in the Scriptures to remain somewhat hidden in the moment. However, after enough coincidences we suddenly wake up and say, "Wow, someone else has had a hand in all of this."

For instance, Hannah was barren. In her sorrow, she went up for a great annual festival at Shiloh. She went to the sanctuary to be by herself and to pray. She was not expecting anyone to take notice of her. The prophet

Eli saw her and thought she was drunk. After she explained, Eli, as much from embarrassment as anything else, blessed her. She became pregnant and brought her child and gave him to Eli to raise. Though giving our child to a prophet seems odd to us, doing what she did was considered a beautiful thing by Israelite culture at the time.

Eli had done a poor job with his children, and they had become arrogant young men. Evidently he learned. The child of Eli's blessing, Hannah's thank offering to him, became Samuel, one of the greatest of the prophets. I encourage you to read the story (1 Sam. 1-4).

Everything about this story can be explained as a coincidence. Yet, looking back, Hannah and Eli saw God's hand. There are times when everything fits together so amazingly and the effects are so unpredictably good that even very secular people will say, "It seems like someone up there really likes me." The response of God's people is "Yes. There really is someone up there that loves you. Embrace that and rejoice."

I cannot say how much I understood at the time about God's love and my friendship with Mrs. Courtney, probably not much. What I did know in my six-year-old way was enough. Thanking God for Mrs. Courtney helped me accept being in America. I came to realize that my mother did not have to know everything I needed. God would provide others to help. Since Mrs. Courtney accepted me, I had hope others would do the same.

For Further Thought or Discussion:
- Who have been the Mrs. Courtneys in your life? What did they give you?
- How have you been able to give simple gifts to someone? What was that like?
- When have you known that there is "someone up there?"

Journal and Share.

Day Three: Some Things about Intercessory Prayer

Because praying for other people puts you in touch with their needs, intercessory prayer feeds your ministry to others. The following five thoughts will help you with your ministry. Let's look at three of them today and two tomorrow.

Make a List: If you do not already keep a prayer list, turn to Appendix D for an example of a form you can use. I make copies off a master and keep them in a binder along with the God Sightings sheets, but in a different section. That works well for most people.

You will probably want to keep some people you pray for in groups, such as your family, and pray for them once a week. Others you may want to keep in front because you want to pray for them every time you pray, like a friend going into the hospital. When the prayer has been answered or the situation is resolved, just draw a line through their name. Add sheets as you need them.

Generally I do not pray for more than 30 people at a time simply because I lose all concentration and begin just to read names. Your limit may be 20 people, or perhaps it is 50. Whatever your limit, it is better to pray for 20 people twice in a day rather than rattle off 60 names just to get through the list.

Intercessory prayer is about addressing God with our concerns for others, not fulfilling some sort of religious obligation. If you start feeling the need to complete a task in too little time, laugh. You are already good at that and do not need practice. Mark where you are and start there the next time you pray.

Making a list helps to prevent us from having to pray the weakest possible prayer, "Lord, I know someone asked me to pray for something just the other day. You know who I mean. Will you take care of it?" That just will not do.

Follow-Up: There is no substitute for knowing that we will talk to someone again about their prayer request. That is good for two reasons: we are more likely to be faithful and they are more likely to feel supported. If we have not been praying, most of us just cannot bring ourselves to say, "I have been praying for your uncle." When we bump into someone at the recycling center, being able to say "How is your uncle?" is a good thing. Faithfulness just feels right. Following up also lets the person who asked us to pray know that they are not alone. Part of intercessory prayer is for us to sustain people by talking to them about their concerns.

Prayer Is a Discipline: Decide how often you are going to pray for others. If you are beginning to develop a discipline, set expectations you can live with. Daily is the biblical norm, but it may take you a while to get there. "The Devil takes particular delight in defeating us with our own best intentions." This old saying has a valid point. If you fail to meet your own expectations, you may begin to avoid prayer entirely. If you find yourself shying away from prayer, try to restart and see what happens. Having to restart is normal.

For Further Thought or Discussion:
- Which of these suggestions concerning intercessory prayer do you already do?
- On which of them you are weak? You may want to practice strengthening that area next week.

Journal and Share.

Day Four: More Things about Intercessory Prayer

Pray Boldly: We are God's children. Martin Luther counseled us to storm the towers of heaven with our prayers. David was very bold in how he spoke to God; even his confessions were very straightforward (Psalm 51). Jesus encourages us to be persistent and bold in our prayers (Luke 11:5-13).

But many of us have been taught to pray differently. Richard Foster took all the prayers in the New Testament and laid them out by type. In reviewing intercessory prayer, he realized that he had been taught an unbiblical form of prayer. He had been taught to close his prayers for others with the words, "yet not my will, but yours be done." These are Jesus' words in his Gethsemane prayer: "Father, if you are willing, take this cup from me, yet not my will, but yours be done" (Luke 22:42). Though Jesus said these words, the context was a prayer for himself in which he was struggling to accept what he hated to accept, the manner of his own death. When Jesus prayed for others, he was very direct. "Be healed," "Father, forgive them," "Open your eyes and see." So Richard Foster reminds us that prayer for others that is truly biblical is prayed directly and without reservation.[3]

Pray as children talk to their parents. I remember one time I wanted to go to the movies. I was afraid my mother would say no. So I hemmed and hawed until my mother said, "Do not pussyfoot around with me. I am your mother. Spit it out. Tell me what you want, then I will tell you what I will do." So I did. Do not pussyfoot around with God. God is your loving Father and you can speak your mind. My mother could say, "Yes," or "No," or "I'll consider that." So can God. Pray boldly. It affirms who you are and who God is.

Expect Change: This flies in the face of the faith assumption of secular people that we live in a "closed universe." In that theory, everything that happens today has a cause in yesterday's happenings and is entirely predictable quite apart from either free will or the reality of God. Life goes on like some giant mechanism, "click click, click click." Why pray if everything is predetermined and nothing can be influenced?

James said that the prayers of a righteous person are effective (James 5:16). Prayer has the power to change things. There you have it. If you pray with the expectation that your prayer makes a difference, you are a poor secularist. If you assert that your prayers can make a difference,

---

[3] Richard Foster, *Celebration of Discipline* (New York: HarＤerＤoＤＤiＤs, 1988), Ｄg. 37.

the overly educated but personally passive keepers of everything currently "politically correct" will tell you, "You are an arrogant fool. Everything is relative. There is no certainty." Jesus, however, will embrace you and go to the Father and advocate your message as being worth consideration.

For Further Thought or Discussion:
- Which of these suggestions concerning intercessory prayer do you already do?
- On which of them are you weak? You may want to practice strengthening that area next week.

Journal and Share.

Day Five: Life among the Methodists

Occasionally we all find ourselves in unexpected places, then discover that we are accepted anyhow. Because I attended a non-denominational seminary, I was outside my denomination's structure for finding a church. At Christmas I contacted the appropriate official and filled out some paperwork. My primary contact called me back in time and said that he had the perfect opportunity for me. Would I mind being lent to the Methodists? He assured me that I would be working under a wonderful, experienced pastor who was a personal friend and a good, Christian man. Besides that, he had graduated from my local denominational seminary and was its alumni association president. "Sure," I said. "Why not?"

I became an ecumenical experiment. The first Sunday that I preached, the text was from the Sermon on the Mount: "Do not worry" (Mt. 6:25-34). I am an expert worrier; God and I had had a few chats about that. My sermon was from the heart and it was biblical. Apparently Methodists worry too. After the service, person after person shook my hand saying things like, "Fine old Methodist sermon," and "The Wesleys would have been proud of you." I gave up trying to explain that I was not a Methodist.

The Christ in them had seen the Christ in me and we were family. The rest was not important. I was accepted among them even though I had been raised in another family of Christians.

For Further Thought or Discussion:
- Have you gone somewhere, expected to be treated like an outsider only to be welcomed? What was that like?
- How do people show each other that they are accepted?
- Whom do you know who would be encouraged by hearing from you?

Journal and Share.

Remember to review your notes from the week and share your insights with a friend. If you are in a group, take your notes to the next meeting.

Week Four:
Lord, Do I Count?

Leaders, make extra copies of all forms.

Before you begin, gather your notebooks, have blank God Sightings forms and index cards. Also have copies of Appendix C, Prayer List or your prayer notebook. Turn to the Appendix D and make a copy of the form, Review of Week __/__/__. Have a pen or pencil.

Say,

In the quiet between each thought, repeat it to yourself silently. Then be still and listen. God is with you. Are you with God? Let us pray:

Begin with prayer. Remember to pause after each thought giving group members opportunity to reflect.

"Present Lord, we offer you our hearts. Come and enter in. You value us. In Christ you left the prerogatives of heaven to live with us. You taught us, you laughed with us and you laid down your life for us and called us friends. Yet within our hearts are voices that doubt our value. At times we convince ourselves that we are small, unimportant and even less than that. We are hungry for your truth. By your Spirit help us to hold that truth in the center of our lives. In Christ's name. Amen."

Pause for a count of at least ten.

God thinks you are valuable. That is huge. Many people stay busy in order to avoid feeling insignificant. They would rather be exhausted than face the question "Do I count for something in this universe?" Without God valuing us, the answer secularism offers is "We are worth about $46 for the chemicals in our body." This answer in all of its forms is a denial of the Good News. God values them and God values you. You do not have to work or play or shop until you drop. You count because you are a child of God.

This week you will learn how to make a periodic review of your life. You will also learn a new way to meditate on the psalms. Cycle Four focuses on love as valuing. The additional material will encourage you to think about valuing in a variety of ways. We grow in wisdom as we learn how to touch others effectively with God's love. You will also find a quick look at the effect of trauma on people's ability to learn how to meditate.

Doing Weekly and Monthly Reviews

We are closing in on a month already. If you are journaling, you now have numerous God sightings. You also have a number of acts of ministry to complete. Some of them you have already done. You may see other acts you choose not to do. Seeing these patterns helps you to become more aware of what some of your strengths and weakness as a minister are. For you, valuing other people may be natural; however, for some people valuing others will be an entirely new field of ministry. Whatever you have learned, you have come a long way in four weeks. That is just great.

Review the following. If you are in a group, take turns reading.

Appendix C is a form headed Review of Week __/__/__. Read and answer the questions.

Looking at where we have been is important. Many people's first realization that God is with them comes from looking back and seeing how perfectly a sequence of events fits together. Their developing awareness of God's presence in the here-and-now is built on the foundation of seeing where God has been with them yesterday. Further, as we look back, we see how intertwined our lives are with others. Pondering the interconnections helps us prepare as we plan our ministry to others.

Finally, we sometimes realize that God has put before us new freedoms or new challenges. Knowing that helps us to cooperate with the activity of the Spirit. We may be more willing to practice new skills until they become familiar. Becoming like Christ means change, and change means practice. It is a good thing to become better at valuing those around us.

When you read your last week's God Sightings journal, direct the first question on the form to your own experience. Do not use the questions to analyze your actions. Rather, pray silently to yourself, "Lord, what do you want me to understand." Listen. Do not try to manage your thoughts. Be aware of what emerges from the clutter of your heart. Allow the Holy Spirit to present you with insights into what is happening in your life. Repeat the process with the other three questions.

The following example may help you understand how to use the review form:

1. Look back over the week. After reviewing the God Sightings you recorded, pray, "Lord, what

are the forms of faithfulness that are easy for me?" Listen.

> I am experiencing more peace. I have more emotional distance from the outcome. The thought that seems to fit is "Make the offer, speak the thought, but do not try to make others change." Last week it was much easier for me to hear others. Though I was more detached, I was able to resonate with their feelings. Oh, yes empathy.

Now review your God Sightings for the week and your ministry acts. Using the form, do your own weekly review.

Four weeks from now, reread all four reviews. Using the same form, think of what you have experienced over the last month. Doing this may help you gain a sense of where God has met you and the direction that God is taking you.

Preparing to Meditate

Remember to open your eyes when you are done. Prepare yourself to meditate by taking your center of awareness from the top of your head to your toes. Start at the top of your head. Be aware of any unnecessary tension around your eyes. Move to your temples. Relax. Move to your ears. Relax. Move the center of your awareness to your neck. You may want to move your head from side to side. Relax. How about your shoulders? Relax. Move down your spine. Relax. Your chest. Relax. Your abdomen. Relax. Your lower back. Relax. Your hips.

This exercise will be difficult for some members of your group so be prepared to sit with and encourage people who are stuck. When the group is done, say,

Have the group pick partners. Say,

Your upper legs. Your knees. Your lower legs. Your ankles. Your feet. Your toes.

Pause for a count of ten. Say,

Repeat each phrase of this prayer silently to yourself, then listen:

"Lord, I seek the presence of the Holy Spirit. In Christ's name. Amen."

Begin by rereading about six God Sightings. Close your eyes and relive one or two of those moments. Where were you? What was happening? When did you become aware of God? When done, open your eyes and relax.

After most people have opened their eyes, say,

Return thanks to God for each experience of his love and for each of your opportunities to love others. When done, share at least one experience with a partner.

After two minutes switch partners.

Scripture

Read,

"O LORD, our Sovereign,
how majestic is your name in all the earth!
You have set your glory above the heavens.
Out of the mouths of babes and infants
you have founded a bulwark
because of your foes, to silence the enemy and the avenger.
When I look at your heavens, the work of your fingers,
the moon and the stars that you have established;
what are human beings that you are mindful of them,
mortals that you care for them?
Yet you have made them a little lower than God, and

crowned them with glory and honor.
You have given them dominion over the works of your
hands;
You have put all things under their feet,
All sheep and oxen,
and also the beasts of the field,
the birds of the air, and the fish of the sea
and whatever passes along the paths of the seas.
O Lord, our Sovereign,
how majestic is your name in all the earth!"

(Psalm 8 NRSV)

Meditation on Scripture

Here is another way to meditate. It is particularly useful with psalms. First, we use our minds to understand the structure of the passage, then we use our hearts to ponder its depths. Psalm 8 is about how God, the Creator of the universe, values each of us.

Have the group open their books to page 61. Review together.

Step One
Psalms typically state their essential content in the first verse or two, then state a conclusion in the last verse or two. The middle portion will have several sections that explore the theme. For instance this psalm begins and ends on the same note, how God's splendor takes our breath away: "O Lord, our Sovereign, how majestic is your name in all the earth!" We can expect the middle of this psalm to explore the majesty of God. For other examples, check out www.godlisteningheart.org.

Step Two

Once we have understood the beginning and the end, we look at the middle. We already have a pretty good idea of what to expect. The central portion of Psalm 8, for instance, is all about the majesty of God. It contains three images around which the entire psalm revolves.

David was sitting on the roof of his palace one evening, the sun was setting and the moon rising and the stars appearing. First, he looked at the wall around the city. The wall was a strong defense. Because of the wall, mothers were sitting outside their homes feeding their babies or rocking them to sleep. Older children were playing. Fathers were at home.

How amazing this was to David. As a young shepherd, he would have been around a campfire at nightfall with a dozen men and the sheep. The coming of the night was a dangerous time. Various large cats and bears had a fondness for sheep and little respect for the shepherds. The shepherds were separated from their wives and mothers. Because the younger children were at home safe with their mothers, they were relative strangers to their own fathers.

How curiously and wonderfully different life was now. David was sitting on the roof of a fine home in a walled city surrounded by families and small children playing. How astonishing God had been in David's life! What amazing things God was doing for the people through David. How majestic is God's name!

Second, David looked at the moon and the stars, the work of God's fingers. How vast God is! How insignificant we are! Martin Luther, reflecting on the same experience of staring into the night sky, said that the first miracle is that God notices that we exist and the second miracle is that, having noticed, he cares. How majestic is his name!

The third set of thoughts and images come from David looking at the fields. He saw the walls, the roads, the lights in the houses, the animals and the olive trees. In his mind's eye he saw the fisherman harvesting the waters and the sailors using the waters to transport goods. God's creative genius is so astonishing. But from the beginning God has given us dominion, the power to shape the environment around us. Though we sometimes make poor use of that power, with it we can do incredible things. How much does God value us? God has made us a little less than the angels. How majestic is his name!

David pondered three things: life with God is amazing; we are so small and God is so immense; God has given us power to shape the world we live in.	*At this point, have the group put their books down.*
Having reviewed the structure of the psalm and gotten some background, meditate on the same psalm with your heart. Begin with prayer.	
"Lord, when have I sat amazed at how you have used me or blessed the people around me?"	*Pray,*
Allow yourself to dwell on that time. Who was involved? Why was the time sweet to you?	*Pause.*

63

"Lord, when was I overwhelmed by your vastness?" Be still and listen.

Pause.

"Lord, have you astonished me when I was looking at the stars, seeing a mountain range or some other experience?"

Pause.

"Lord, the universe is so vast. How can you care?"

Pause.

"In the Sermon on the Mount Jesus referred to the fact we are created to have dominion. We can affect the world around us and cooperatively create societies. Jesus urged us to consider the birds of the air, for they neither sow nor reap nor store away into barns. Yet our Heavenly Father feeds them. Do you believe that you are of greater value to God than a bird?" (Mt. 6:25a-26).

"Is David right? Does Jesus make sense? Can you affirm this psalm?"

Pause.

"O Lord, our Sovereign, how majestic is your name in all the earth."

Pause.

Say,

Open your eyes. Make whatever notes seem appropriate to you.

When done say,

The author's website has other examples of sorting out the main thoughts of a psalm, then meditating on them: go to www.godlisteningheart.org.

The Fourth Cycle of Exercises: Valuing

"Give me a God-listening heart" (1 Kings 3:9 TM).

Exercise One: Listening to the Voice of the God Who Values Us

Relax. Take the center of your awareness to any part of your body in which you have tension and release it. Breathe in normally. Remember to repeat each of these prayers silently to yourself.

"Lord, do I count to you?"

"Lord, am I important to you?"

"Lord, how do I know that you think I am valuable?"
Listen without conscious control.

What pops into your awareness? Is it true? If not, keep listening for the voice within that affirms your value. Open your eyes when you are done.

After recording in your notebook what you heard, saw or felt, the next step is to look at your current experience with God.

Exercise Two: Listening for the Gifts We Receive

Relax, take a deep breath, let it out. Breathe in normally. Remember to repeat each of these prayers silently to yourself.

Say,
Pause.

Pause.

Pause.

When most have opened their eyes, say,

After the group makes notes say,

Pause.

"When during the last day have I seen you value me?" Listen.

Pause.

"Lord, you have shown me in Jesus Christ that I count. Now help me see that in my life today." Listen.

Pause.

"Lord, how do I know from my experience that I count?" Listen.

Make notes of your God sightings, then thank God for being in your life.

After the group makes notes say,

Let us refocus our attention on others we know. Take a deep breath, then let it out. Breathe in normally.

Exercise Three: Listening for the Gifts We Give

Say,

"Lord, in the last 24 hours, where was I when I showed another that they were worthwhile?" Listen quietly for the conversation within.

Pause.

"Lord, what was going on when I showed another that they counted?" Listen.

Pause.

"Lord, you were willing to die for us. What was I willing to do to value another?" Listen.

Pause.

When done, write down one or two examples of how you have blessed another with the same sort of love you have met in God. You may have valued them or may have loved them in other ways. Thank God for the privilege of offering blessings, gifts of love, to people who are a part of your life.

Let us refocus our attention by praying for others, then asking God for guidance in our personal ministry.

After the group makes notes, say,

Exercise Four: Listening for God's Guidance for Our Ministry to Others

Pray through your prayer list. Make notes on an index card or a Memos from God form to carry with you during the day.

Say,

Relax, take a deep breath, then let it out. Breathe in normally.

Pause. When most eyes are open, say,

"Lord, is there someone you would have me value today?" Listen.

Pause.

"Lord, whom do you want me to build up today?" Listen.

Pause.

"Lord, whom do I know who needs to be recognized?" Listen.

Pause.

When done, give yourself a few minutes to write down on an index card the people and acts that God brought to your heart today.

Discernment

When most are done, say,

This list of acts can serve as intentional blessings by which you enrich your ministry to others. This may even teach you new dimensions of love. Thank God for each of these people and possibilities.

Pause.

Reflect on the spirit behind each act to see if it is right. If you sense that something other than loving others through valuing them or understanding them or accepting them is going on, circle the act.

When you have finished reviewing each act, return to the questionable items and ask God to show you what he wants you to understand about each act. You may discover that your discomfort has to do with not recognizing it as an act of ministry. Sometimes you have never done something like that before. In either case, give it a try. If you have no resolution of why you are uncomfortable with it, skip it and do the others. Return daily with the God-listening prayer, "Lord, what do you want me to understand about this act?" God will help you and perhaps even amaze you in time. Be patient and consistent.

When most are done, say,

Pull out your index cards from the last several weeks. Note which acts of ministry you relish. I hope you remembered to put down both the date you were given the thought and the date you did it. Make a mental note of the ones you have not done yet and ask for God's help in getting them done.

When most are done, say,

This completes the fourth cycle of meditation and your first periodic review. That is a lot to do, and it is great that with God's help you are getting it done. In the Going Deeper section are four days of additional material you may find useful. I encourage you to work through as many of these as you can. If you have the time, also pick up any you did not work through in previous weeks. Perhaps you want to meditate in the morning and use this material in the evening before you go to bed.

If time permits, take a break then share from the Going Deeper offerings. Close with prayer.

Going Deeper

Day One: Chicks and Rocks and Hand Puppets for Christmas

One way to value another is to give up something that is dear to you. My younger sister Elsie is and always has been a good-hearted person. When she was five, she was too young to have an allowance. At Christmas she wanted to join in the gift giving. So what was Elsie to do? She looked through her favorite possessions. She wrapped them up and gave them to us, her three brothers. I got a type of quartz crystal called a geode, my older brother got little yellow wooden chick figures from last Easter's basket and my younger brother got a hand puppet. We were speechless.

Just as we began to snigger at each other, Mother hugged her and thanked her and told her she was beautiful. She turned to the three of us with one of those faces that says, "Hush up and right now!" My mother said, "She has given you the things she prizes the most. How lovely."

Now when I close my eyes, I can still see the crystals thrusting toward the jagged, hollow center of the geode. They say, "Jamie, you count to your sister." That is still precious.

The Scriptures teach that we have the endowments we have because we reflect the nature of God (Gen. 1:27) even though we are fallen and God's image is obscured (Romans 5:12-19). We are many things, both noble and dreadful. Even as children we are capable of uncalculating generosity. In those acts we capture quite exquisitely something of the nature of the God we worship. I did not recognize that immediately. My mother's guidance was a help, I am sure. I think, however, that as an adult we can see the beauty of simple generosity in part because it is so easy to forget generosity.

For Further Thought or Discussion:
- Today, who showed you that you counted?

- How does God tell you that you count?
- How can a person show another person that they count?

Journal and Share.

Day Two: Feeling Insignificant and Being Insignificant.

At times most people feel pretty insignificant. Many managers at work do not value their subordinates. Being fired or laid off hardly uplifts us. Occasionally a friend decides to drop our relationship. Some parents are so absorbed with themselves that they forget to celebrate their children. Other people conclude that their fathers or mothers do not care about them very much as a result of a divorce. For all these reasons and more, you may believe that God loves you, but have trouble hearing God say, "I value you." The noise inside your heart can drown out God's truth.

Though you may feel insignificant, that does not make you insignificant. Your personal feelings do not alter God's nature. You count because God values you. Tough experiences may mean that you have more trouble than most at seeing how God values you and why you are important to other people. Hard times, however, do not change the truth about God and our relationship to him.

> *And we (Christians) know that in all things God works for the good of those who love him, who have been called according to his purpose. ...If God is for us, who can be against us? He who did not spare his own Son, but gave him up for us all—how will he not also, along with him, graciously give us all things?* (Romans 8:28 31-32).

If you are one who doubts your own value as a person, I hope I never promised you that this was easy. The point is that it is true. God values you, so it becomes your responsibility and your joy to look for those experiences that affirm the truth. It is by God's power that you can live the truth in your relationship to others.

If you already know that you are valued, that is terrific. These same exercises will help you share that knowledge with others through practical acts of love.

For Further Thought or Discussion:
- What is your favorite way of saying, "You count!"?
- Who is easy for you to affirm?
- Who is difficult and why? Is the reason really important?

Journal and Share.

Day Three: Trauma and Meditation

Meditation can be a very powerful aid in coping with trauma. In crisis many people cry out for validation. Learning how to meditate in the middle of a crisis may be difficult. I was just talking to a woman whose husband died in an automobile accident. They had been married eight years. She has three children and a part-time job that pays minimum wage. Of the money she received from his business life insurance, most went to retiring debt on cars and a boat and several charge cards. She is in the midst of selling assets she does not need or cannot afford.

Although she believes that there is a loving God somewhere, she says she is not sure where to find him. Though she does not realize it, I suspect that she is angry with God. Therefore, she does not want to hear about how loving God is, especially how valuable God thinks she and her children are.

Knowing just how hollow words can be, I put her in touch with a woman who has gone through something similar. This woman has a marvelous ministry to people who are in the midst of a crisis. Today's hurt is preparation for tomorrow's ministry.

Besides referring her to a wonderful woman who has seen hard times herself, I suggested she use an exercise to remember to thank God for what is right in her life. Now, she readily acknowledges the joy of her children, supportive friends and a loving church community. She knows that others treasure her.

When a person senses her or his value to others while remembering what is right in life, that person has opened up to a powerful combination. Personally, I do not attempt anything as elaborate as these cycles with people in crisis until they are well grounded in what is right in their lives. As she remembers what is right and holds fast to one or more positive relationships, in time God will help her cope with the rest. When we are together, she talks, I listen.

For Further Thought or Discussion:
- Have you been through a really bad time? How did you cope?
- When a parent is having trouble with one child, what is the effect of remembering to value the other children?
- Does thanksgiving help people remember that much of life is good and that it is important to affirm that?

Journal and Share.

Day Four: New Beginnings

If we want to be like Jesus, we need to value the people we work with. I was the first salesperson to be hired by Bill Pritchard, as good a businessperson as I have known. A very bright and a decent human being, he has been incredibly successful. No one is perfect, however, including Bill. Pleased to have found me, he called the staff together and told them he was hiring an Ivy League graduate who knew nothing about the insurance business. Unfortunately, money was short, so instead of the staff getting a raise, they got me.

"Help him succeed," Billy said, "since this is an important step forward in the development of the agency. He can take us places you can't, so don't worry about not having a raise." Well, he did not exactly say it that way, but that is what his staff heard.

I could feel the hostility as I walked in the door. I knew that graduates of Ivy League colleges are considered by many to be "Big People," even the worried, ignorant ones. I knew that I had to let everyone in the office know that I thought they counted, that in my book there were no "Little People."

That was easy enough to do. There is nothing like the truth. First, I was unable to function at all without their help. Also, my coworkers were people God cared enough for to leave the splendor of heaven. If God decided to come and dwell with us, valuing those we work with reflects Christ's ministry. Jesus was prepared to die for us. I think it makes sense to die spiritually by swallowing pride and the desire for affirmation and by taking the initiative to honor others.

In time my coworkers accepted me. Taking the initiative to value them helped, I am sure. The fact they put their disappointment aside was a statement about their basic fairness and professionalism. I am still grateful to them for who they were and for the wisdom of our faith, which is such a help.

For Further Thought or Discussion:
- Think back to a time in your life when another person at work told you that you counted. What was going on? What difference did that make?
- Yesterday, how did God tell you that you count? Answer from your experience, not theological language.
- Who in your acquaintance needs to know that he or she counts?

Journal and Share.

Remember to do a weekly review. Share with a friend. If you are in a group, take your notes with you to the next meeting.

73

Week Five:
Lord, Can I Succeed?

*Leaders, supply
extra forms.*

*Pausing after each
thought, pray,*

**Before getting into the material, take the time to
collect your notebooks, have a pencil or pen. Have
blanks of all forms in the appendixes on hand and
organize your Memos from God by date.**

*"Amazing God, you who created work as a reflection of
your nature, help us to value our ability to modify the
world around us rightly. Teach us the difference between
business and busyness. In Christ's name. Amen."*

This week you will learn a way to review your
Memos from God in order to grow in faithfulness.
You may discover that reviewing what you are already doing well will encourage you to grow in
ministry. Making small changes to honor God allows him to build confidence into our futures. This
week's cycle focus is on success, and the additional
material will encourage you to look at aspects of
your life that you may not always remember to relate to God.

Reviewing Your Ministry

Get your Memos from God or Ministry Lists or whatever you call them. If you have not already done so, arrange your lists in order from the oldest to the newest. As you review them, consider what was easy and what you have avoided doing.

What sorts of ministry do you do almost immediately? What takes weeks? What is still undone even though it came to you in prayer and would reflect the love of Jesus Christ?

Most of us find that we eagerly do certain things but are "just too busy" to do things that are new to us, are uncomfortable for us or involve people we do not know well. These ministries we are reluctant to do represent the growing edge of our personal ministry. If you discover a pattern of ministry you avoid, ask God, "Lord, show me what you want me to understand about my reluctance." Then hush up and wait.

You may have to ask for God's guidance several days in a row or even longer. Keep it up. The results can be remarkably helpful.

Here is an example of the sorts of things you may learn about yourself. George would not write notes to people. He discovered that the reason for that was that his father had not written notes. As a child he concluded that note writing was for women. That is not much of a reason to refuse to care for others in such a simple way, but it was vintage George.

Have the group choose partners. Say,

Pause.

Pause, allowing up to three minutes. Say,

Pause.

I have discovered that when God puts acts before me that I do not want to do, I will do that same thing I do with my wife. I stop listening (praying) and get busy with other things. As we become more honest and consistent in our relationship to God we begin to grow spiritually and develop wisdom about others and ourselves. I look forward to you discovering areas of avoidance and working them through. God wants to set you free and allow you to enjoy faithfulness. The service of the Lord is sweet and usually a great joy.

Preparing to Meditate

Say,

Prepare yourself to meditate by taking your center of awareness down from the top of your head to your toes, relaxing each major muscle group as you do.

Give the group three minutes to relax. Pray,

"By your Spirit, Lord, be with me and help me to hear what you have to say and to follow where you lead me. In Christ's name. Amen."

Begin by rereading six or so of your God sightings. Spend about five minutes remembering the moments. Do that in whatever manner is natural for you. Thank God.

Provide a time of sharing.

Scripture

Read.

No testing has overtaken you that is not common to everyone. God is faithful, and he will not let you be tested beyond your strength, but with the testing he will also provide the way out so that you may be able to endure it (1 Cor. 10:13 NRSV).

Pause.

Meditation on Scripture

"Lord, show me yourself through these words."

Pray,
Pause.

"Lord, what do you want me to see?"

Pause.

"Lord, I want to be open to you."

Jot down your thoughts briefly.

Say,

Give the group a few minutes.

The Fifth Cycle of Exercises: Succeeding

"Give me a God-listening heart" (1 Kings 3:9).

Exercise One: God is Eager for Your Success as a Person

Relax. Check for and release any unnecessary tension.

Say,
Pause.

"Lord, can I succeed in life?" Listen without conscious control.

Pause.

"Lord, do you consider me capable of success?" Listen.

Pause.

"Lord, did you create me so I can succeed?" Listen.

Say,

Jot down what came to you. Record qualified or negative answers in your notebook and later ask God what you are to understand about them. Remember, only the voices that say that you are capable of success represent the truth. This is a difficult exercise for two reasons. For some reason most people have disassociated success from their personal faith. They believe that God is indifferent to their effectiveness In life, especially their work. This is not true, but a common view. Additionally, many people identify themselves with their accomplishments. We are not human doings. We are human beings. The voices that doubt our ability to be effective represent conclusions, opinions or the results of experiences that have never been resolved in the light of God's truth.

There are periods in many people's lives in which they seriously doubt that they are successful at anything. Over time you have failed at many things. Do not be concerned if you hear negative answers. The focus is to learn to hear the truth in the midst of your internal conversations. The truth is that God has a purpose for you at which you can succeed.

Exercise Two: Listening for the Gifts We Receive

Pray,
Pause.

"Lord, where was I when I was successful?" Listen.

Pause.

"Lord, what was happening when I knew you were touching me with success?" Listen.

Pause.

"Lord, when did I know that I had done a fine job and that you were pleased?" Listen.

Pause.

Make notes of anything that comes to you. Take time to thank God for being in your life, then go to the next exercise.

78

Exercise Three: Listening for the Gifts We Give

Relax, take a deep breath, then let it out. Breathe in normally.

"Lord, show me how I have helped another succeed in the last day." Listen.

"Lord, what was happening when I showed another how they can succeed?" Listen.

"Lord, when did I celebrate another's success in the last day or two?" Listen.

Make a few notes on how you have blessed another. Thank God for the privilege of offering gifts of love to others.

Exercise Four: Listening for God's Guidance for Our Ministry to Others

Pray through your prayer list. Open your eyes and look up when you are done.

Having prayed for others, ask God to show you people you can love and acts you can do. Relax, take a deep breath, then let it out. Breathe in normally. Let it out. Release any unnecessary tension.

"Lord, whom would you have me encourage today?"

Say,

Pause a minute.

Pause three minutes.

Pause.

Pause.

Pause up to three minutes.

Say,

Pause until the group is done or three minutes have passed.

Pray,

Pause.

Listen.
"Lord, so many people think they are failures. Whose

Pause.

success can I note and celebrate today?" Listen.

"Lord, who in my network of relationships needs some-

Pause.
Give the group up
to three minutes.

thing I can offer in order to get the job done?" Listen.

Jot down the people and acts that God brought to your heart today. Thank God for each of these people and possibilities.

Discernment

Say,

Look over your list of ministry acts. Read Paul's description of love in 1 Corinthians 13:4-7. Test your possible acts against Paul's words. Will the things you are considering express a spirit that is patient or kind? Is the spirit free from envy, boasting, pride and rudeness? Are you seeking an advantage for yourself

Pause five
minutes.
Say,

or for the other person? Is the spirit behind the act free from irritation and free from remembered hurt?

For each act where the answer is yes, go do it. May you experience the joy of being God's hands and heart on the earth.

This completes the cycle. How are you doing for time? The temptation is to write too much for each God sighting. Ordinary daily experiences are valuable as they add up. Turning points are etched in our hearts forever. If an event is really important to your spiritual life, God will keep it fresh in your heart and you will remember. Be brief with your notes.

The quickest way to become ineffective is to treat everything like it is terribly important. Do not analyze things to death. Otherwise, you will never seem to have the time to do these exercises. The truth may be that you are having trouble trusting God to guide you to spend time on the one or two situations or people who occasionally require it.

If you are a member of a group, remember to take

If time permits, take a break then share from the Going Deeper offerings from last week. Close with prayer.

your notes with you.

Going Deeper

You have five days of material this week. If you only get three done, remember that three beats zero. Do a weekly review. Pay attention to ministry acts you are struggling with. Ask God to show you what he wants you to understand each day until you gain clarity. It is often helpful to discuss this with a friend or pastor.

Day One: Reflections on the Passage

We often fail to succeed because our greatest temptation is to continue to do what we find familiar and fun, even if we know we will end up hurting. In a manner of speaking, we fall in love with our temptations. As we dwell on them in our imaginations, they seem bigger, stronger and more irresistible.

We sometimes collude to fail with our friends. If you tell a friend that no one could possibly resist their temptation, perhaps they will tell you the same about one of yours. So people try to look reasonable and even respectable, then do what they know at some level is wrong, then try to engineer cheap forgiveness so they maintain their relationships even as they waste time, money, opportunity and goodwill through poor choices.

Jesus Christ came to set us free and Paul shows us how to claim our freedom. In one verse (1 Cor. 10:13) he both deflates our rather bizarre notions about how awful our temptations are and reminds us that God is faithful. So when we are faced with temptation, Paul reminds us that we should stop kidding ourselves. Do not dwell on how huge the temptation is. Instead, ask God to show us the way out. "God is faithful."

For Further Thought or Discussion:
- Make a list of common temptations. What is good about them? What are the problems?
- What are common excuses people give in order to avoid looking for the way out?

Journal and Share.

Day Two: A Second Huge Passage on the Subject of Temptation, Sin and Failure

> *Blessed is anyone who endures temptation. Such a one has stood the test and will receive the crown of life that the Lord has promised to those who love him. No one, when tempted, should say, "I am being tempted by God," for God cannot be tempted by evil and he himself tempts no one. But one is tempted by one's own desire, being lured and enticed by it; then, when that desire has conceived, it gives birth to sin, and that sin, when it is fully grown, gives birth to death. Do not be deceived, my beloved* (James 1:12-16 NRSV).

Many people feel they have failed because they have been tempted. We are powerless to avoid temptation. Even Jesus was tempted. The fact of temptation is not, in and of itself, important. With God's help we do not have to act on it.

If we try to avoid the thought or resolve to ignore it or resist it, we are in trouble. The more we try to avoid the temptation, the more ways it pops up in our soul. Instead, we need to substitute a positive alternative to focus on. At a conference I met a Chinese pastor from Hong Kong. I will call him Lee. Part of the focus of the conference was dealing with temptation. When tempted, Lee said he usually had a fleeting picture of some pleasure. For instance, he was addicted to gambling. When tempted, Lee would see himself squatting in a backroom with other men throwing dice.

Since Lee was tempted through daydreams, he sought to offer his imagination to God. He created a place in his heart based on Psalm 23:2 "...he leads me beside still waters." He pictured himself sitting with Jesus beside Hong Kong harbor on a lovely sunny day. Rather than allowing his imagination to fill up and dwell on the pleasures of gambling, he turns his mind's eye to Jesus sitting beside him.

Once fixed on Jesus, he asks, "Lord what was it you wanted of me today?" He turned from the temptation and substituted something positive related to his ministry. This is a powerful combination, since trying to resist the thought only intensifies it for most people.

On a flight to Chicago, I met a Jesuit who explained to me that he takes an annual retreat based on Ignatus of Loyola's spiritual exercises. The exercises are a series of 13 meditations based on the Bible and dealing with the process of Jesus' crucifixion. Between retreats, he keeps the exercises vivid by reviewing one of them several times each day. When tempted, he thinks about the Crucifixion. He said, "Comparing the surpassing value of the Crucifixion to the flawed joy of sin empties temptation of its power."

Another way to disengage from the tempting thought or image is to sing a favorite hymn to ourselves. For some people, imagination is not a significant help, but music has great power. One friend of mind said that when tempted, he visits his parents' graves. He just senses their presence and that of God at those times. Doing that shifts his attention from the temptation to God. Another person I know makes it a point to bake cookies when he gets home. It reminds him of the value of God's blessing through family and reminds him that giving into his personal temptations would damage those relationships.

However you do it, the principle behind all of these exercises is the same. Disengage from the temptation as soon as you recognize it. Turn your attention to God by substituting something of positive value in its place.

For Further Thought or Discussion:
- What sort of exercise is likely to help you?
- Why not try it out for a week? Journal about your experience and discuss the effect of practicing a specific way of managing temptation with a friend.

Day Three: The Fire Tower

To succeed we have to use our God-given abilities. If we convince ourselves that we will fail anyhow, we do not even try. I had the good fortune to belong to a fine Boy Scout troop as a child. Once a year, our district had a camporee for all the local troops. Each year there was a different theme. One year troops all over Louisville, Kentucky, were to learn how to build a large wooden structure by lashing sticks and logs together. Our scoutmaster announced that our troop was going to build a fire tower. It would have a ladder, a platform and a rail all around. To make this tower, we had to go to a park, find appropriate materials, then learn how to lash wood together using the right knots.

We were skeptical. We whined a lot. We whined that the wood would be too heavy. We whined that we would never be able to do all that tying in time. We whined that it would fall over. Our scoutmaster said, "Oh, come along now. I know you boys and I know you can do it. You will enjoy it and be proud of yourselves."

The next Thursday, the seven of us who made up the Wolf Patrol marched into the park looking for a 14-foot log in good condition, and various other pieces of wood. The other patrols had other assignments. Before long, one of us found the perfect log. We dragged it back and then began to learn the knots used in lashing. We tied and untied until the knots were familiar. One night close to the camporee we arrived for our troop meeting. The wood from all the patrols was gathered there. "Now boys," our scoutmaster said, "tonight we are going to build our fire tower and take it down."

Each patrol assembled different parts. In less than 45 minutes there was a 14-foot tall fire tower on the side lawn of the Highland Methodist Church. It was beautiful. The junior assistant scoutmaster scampered up first. In three weeks, the impossible had become simple. We were amazed to discover that this seemingly overwhelming project was not only easy but fun. Don't panic, think it through, break it down, learn what you have to do and do it. I always remember that experience when

I am tempted to say, "Jamie, it just cannot be done."

Fear causes us to forget our past, especially the times we thought we could not but overcame. Turn to the Scriptures. When either God or an angel appears to people, the common greeting is "Fear not." Journaling and returning thanks for success are tremendous helps to storing up moments of success in spite of anxiety. Instead of embracing failure as the only reasonable option, those memories can help us apply God's confidence to the possibilities of our lives.

For Further Thought or Discussion:
- When did God bring you through a difficult time?
- When have you been surprised by the ease with which people who organize themselves can do the seemingly impossible?
- Is there something in your life that you are nervous about? Rather than saying, "I can't do that," why not ask God, "Is there a way that I can get the job done?"

Journal and Share.

Day Four: The Teacher Who Became a Real Estate Agent

Sometimes we need a change if we are going to succeed as a person. Most of us start careers before we know what God has prepared us to do well. Years ago a member of my church quit teaching and became a real estate agent. Charlie was just not cut out to be an elementary school teacher.

Many people hate the sales process so much that they would rather have a root canal than actually do everything that sales requires. Charlie was apparently an exception. He loved meeting people. He liked houses a lot. He had a good feel for what people were looking for in a house. He accepted the fact that he would only make a sale sometimes but enjoyed the attempt to close each sale. He honestly felt that even when he did not make a sale he could make a friend by helping people determine what they really wanted.

Charlie was in a prayer group I led. One night he said that he was becoming discouraged. "I work hard for six to eight weeks, get a couple of listings, have sales that are nearly happening, then something happens. I get exhausted and just kind of poop out for a week or two. Then I have to start all over."

I imagined sitting next to Jesus. I was asking him what he wanted me to say to Charlie. We can use our imaginations like that because our minds work on several levels at once. When I do this, I actually hear people better because the focus on Jesus takes my focus off of me and puts it on the other person. I am also reminded that the person I am thinking about is a child of God, my brother or sister in Christ.

A thought came to me. I knew somehow that Jesus wanted Charlie to know that he needed to work for a quarter, 13 weeks, then take two weeks off rather than work for six and take one week off. To me, that seemed like an odd thing for Jesus Christ to want me to say to Charlie. Perhaps it was just some stray thought I said to myself. After all, I knew that I was imagining Jesus. Perhaps I was just imagining the thought. The thought was hardly religious.

It has been my experience, however, that another of the promises of the Bible is true. When we do not know what to say, God will give us the words (John 14:26). Since these words came to me in prayer and I could see no reason not to speak them, I looked at Charlie and said, "Why not take two weeks off every quarter rather than one each six weeks?"

Charlie looked surprised, then confused, then smiled and said, "You're right. I know that I am absent too frequently. I lose momentum. It never occurred to me that I could give the time back to my family that way." Charlie reorganized his schedule so that he was off from the second week in August until the middle of September and from about Thanksgiving until the middle of February. He made himself available for the rest of the year. Within two months, Charlie won a prize for closing the most sales in his agency.

Charlie was thrilled. He thought I was a genius. I told him that the thought came as a gift in prayer. Since he believed in a God who loves us actively, I explained that I had listened for the leading of the Holy Spirit. I told him that the idea "came to me" and was not something I thought up. I confessed that I was tempted to say nothing because the words were much too secular for God. I remembered how often Jesus talked about money and used examples from the business world. I knew that God loved Charlie and his family and wanted Charlie to succeed. God put me there and gave me a few words. I had the privilege of helping my friend. Ministry can be a beautiful thing. I invite you to join with those who acknowledge that a loving God is active in our lives and say, "Thank you."

For Further Thought or Discussion:
- Do you sometimes realize things that you know you cannot really know, but they are just the right things to say or do? Remember one of those moments. Did it feel like you were given a gift to be shared with another or did it seem like a fortunate accident?
- When has God challenged your notion of what is "religious" by showing you what actually blesses others?

Journal and Share.

Day Five: My Turn to Struggle

God desires our success as a person in all departments of our lives. That does not mean he wants us all to be millionaires, but he gave most of us talents and interests and wants us to use them in contributing in some way to a prosperous society that can care for each of its citizens. Though age, health, native ability or temperament limit some of us, the limits caused by false beliefs are much more common.

In 1988 I moved to Victor, N.Y., as a part owner-manager of an agency with gross revenues of about $1.5 million. As insurance agencies go, that is about average for a one-owner insurance agency.

Over the next four years, all the bad things that could happen did. Our gross revenue was down by a third. In 1993 the senior partner died. In 1995 I bought out my partners and went on my own. By 1998 I had built the agency up to were it had to be for me to live comfortably. Then I lost my largest account. After all that effort I was back to the bottom in gross revenue.

So there I was in the winter of 1998 with my retirement invested in a failing business. I had a new computer system, a slick personnel manual, great systems and neat files, but I was losing three times more business each year than I was adding. I would be out of business in another three years.

I took my concerns to prayer. I hate to admit it, but I really did think that God would take care of my soul and I would take care of my business. It was not until I was desperate that it occurred to me that God might have an opinion worth listening to. So I prayed a God-listening prayer: "Lord, what do you want me to understand about my business's future?" I prayed and meditated for nearly a month.

One morning I realized I was getting an answer: "Sell."

"Well," I thought, "That's me talking to myself." I wanted God's input.

The next day I prayed again, and again I heard, "Sell."

Though I wanted God's guidance, the word "sell" was not on my list of acceptable answers. I did the only thing that made sense. I stopped talking to God about my agency. As I said above, sometimes when I hear in prayer things I do not want to accept, I just avoid God for a while.

---

[4] Author's note: This is my amplification, not a part of the original text.

tire family and others have benefited in ways I could not have even imagined to pray for. As Jesus said, "Your heavenly Father knows you need them (food, clothing, security and the rest[4]). But seek first his kingdom and his righteousness, and all these things will be given to you as well" (Mt. 6:32-33).

---

[4] Author's note: This is my amplification, not a part of the original text.

Prayer for Busy People

For Further Thought or Discussion:
- Many people avoid change because change means acknowledging a dread. Change also means attempting something new. Many people find that hard also. What has your experience been?
- Is there some dread that holds you back from using your God-given talents? If so, why not hand over that part of your life to God's leading? When I handed over my fear that I might not be important enough to succeed in business, God handled my dread far more appropriately than I ever did. God is just wiser than we are.

Journal and Share.

Remember to do a weekly review and look over your acts of ministries for any you are avoiding. Ask God to show you what you are to understand about your avoidance. Share with a friend. If you are a part of a group, bring your notes to the next meeting.

Several months later I prayed about my agency again. I guess I hoped that God had something different to say. When I got to my business in my meditations, I heard, "Jamie, I will love you whether you fail in business or succeed, but I can use your witness more effectively if you succeed." I was so stunned I had to pay attention.

I admitted to myself that I was afraid and remembered that fear does not generally come from God. In the counsels of my fear I was sure that no one would buy insurance from me because I was so insignificant. In the universe of insurance I just did not count, or so I thought at the time. So why spend the money and the time on marketing?

I tested the spirit of that thought and realized that it could not come from God. It might be true that I would not succeed in spite of my best efforts, but the problem was not that I was too unimportant. Jesus looks at each one of us and says, "You are worth dying for. This is your Creator speaking, the one that set the stars in the heavens. You count." To also believe that I was too insignificant to succeed denies what Jesus says. Someone is wrong here, either the spirit of my fear counseling inaction or Jesus Christ saying "You are OK." I voted for Jesus.

Somehow I knew that Jesus would be with me as I changed my habits. One of his names is Emmanuel and I sensed that Jesus was saying, "Do what you need to do to succeed and remember I am Emmanuel, God with you" (Mt. 1:23). So I wrote the word "Emmanuel" on sticky notes and put one on my computer at home and another at work.

This story has a happy ending. Accepting God's assurance rather than my dread has been a very good decision. With God's leadership, my en-

Week Six:
Lord, Am I Forgiven?

*Leaders, provide
blank forms.*

**Before you begin, gather your notes, blank forms
and have something to write with.**

*Begin with prayer.
Pause after each
thought.*

*"Loving God, you judge rightly the intent of our hearts.
You know the difference between mistakes and intentional harm. You delight in our best and, in spite of our
worse, you seek to have a relationship with us. We are
both astonished and humbled. When we are in need of
forgiveness, help us to be quick to ask and willing to
change. In Christ's name. Amen."*

Pause.

God forgives you. For many, that is the best possible news. Without knowing that, people will use
busyness to avoid recognizing how they feel about
themselves. The result is a lot of unfocused energy
spent on an endless variety of tasks. Having said
that, not all distractions result from avoidance.
Many distractions can be dealt with quickly and
easily. Getting rid of them first makes it easier to
manage deeper distractions.

The readings in Going Deeper deal with hearing another's confession. Read them and make them your
own. Someone you know or will know needs your
ears, your heart and your assurance of forgiveness to

escape the prison of their past. You cannot give a more valuable gift than the gift of a listening heart.

Coping with Distraction

No one can address the issue of forgiveness or any of the other important spiritual issues if they are distracted. In order to reduce distractions, I have made this approach to meditation as simple as I could. You have complete directions for the cycles and the forms to help you organize your experience. The mechanics should present no problem.

Review the following. If you are with others, take turns reading.

Additionally, you have an exercise based on Psalm 23 to calm your soul and two additional ways to build a quiet center. You can ask a God-listening question but will have days in which you will think about something else entirely. After posing a particular question three times and moving through a couple of steps in the cycle, you will discover that you are either meditating, or are so full of different thoughts and concerns that you cannot focus your thoughts. I encourage you to be gentle with yourself. Everyone who meditates experiences days their hearts are so full they cannot listen.

When you discover yourself having one of those times, ignore the plan for the day and ask God to show you what you need to understand about the things that keep on pressing into your awareness.

At other times you will be distracted because of a problem in your relationships with others. Jesus said that God often prevents people from coming to him if they have unresolved problems with someone else (Mt. 5: 21-26). You may have to address your relationships first, then return to your prayers.

If necessary, straighten up, take the phone off the hook or do anything else necessary to minimize external distractions.

There is another common reason for distraction. Most people have trouble meditating when they get behind at work or if the house is a mess. If you sense that God is saying clean up the kitchen or your desk, that may not be a distraction. You just might have to take care of the clutter in your exterior life before the clutter in your head slows down. Perhaps you have not had enough sleep. Exercise is important. Too much alcohol will destroy anyone's ability to meditate. A decent diet helps all mental functioning including meditation. Christians commit themselves to a life of order and moderation because it protects our ability to relate to each other and to God.

Preparing to Meditate

Say,

Prepare yourself to meditate by taking your center of awareness down from the top of your head to your toes, relaxing each major muscle group as you do.

After two minutes, pray, pausing after each thought.

"Lord, I am grateful for so much. I would thank you and love others in your name. By the Holy Spirit, remind me of what you want me to think about. In Christ's name. Amen."

Say,

Reread six or so God sightings. Recall those moments and thank God for them. If you have begun to speed up, remember that there is no such thing as speed meditation. You can always stop and resume again later today or even tomorrow. God will still be there.

Share. After two minutes switch. Pause two minutes.

Scripture

You see, at just the right time, when we were still power-less, Christ died for the ungodly. Very rarely will anyone die for a righteous man, though for a good man someone might possibly dare to die. But God demonstrates his own love for us in this: While we were still sinners, Christ died for us (Romans 5:6-8 NIV).

"Lord, what sticks out in this passage for me?"

What do you hear? What do you see? What do you remember? What jumps out at you? If nothing is coming or your mind is wandering, pray, "Lord, what would you have me consider?"

"Lord, what is your word to me?"

Jot down your thoughts briefly.

Read.

Pause.

Pause.

Pause.

Pause.

Allow up to three minutes for note taking.

The Sixth Cycle of Exercises: Forgiveness

"Give me a God-listening heart" (1 Kings 3:9 TM).

Exercise One: Listening for the Truth

For the next week we will focus on the role of forgiveness in love. Relax and allow your heart to be calm.

"Lord, am I forgiven?" Listen to what emerges without conscious effort.

Say,

Pause.

Pause.

Pause.

"Lord, do you forgive me?" Listen.

Pause.

"Lord, am I acceptable to you?" Listen.

What came to your mind? Is it consistent with the statement "For God did not send his Son into the world to condemn the world, but to save the world through him" (John 3:17)? Focus attention on how God's forgiveness affects us. Write down your answer(s) and thank God for being willing to forgive.

Pause up to two minutes.

Exercise Two: Listening for the Gifts We Receive

Say,

Relax, take a deep breath, and let it out. Breathe in normally. Pray to yourself, "Where was I when I experienced your forgiveness recently?" Listen.

Pause.

"Lord, when did I feel your forgiveness yesterday?" Listen.

Pause.

"Lord, show me how you forgave me." Listen.

Pause.

Make your notes and thank God for forgiveness.

Pause up to two minutes.

Exercise Three: Listening for the Gifts We Give

Say,
Pause.

Take a deep breath, then let it out. Breathe normally.

"Show me where I have assured another that they are forgiven." Listen.

Pause.

"Lord, what was happening when I forgave another?"
Listen.

Pause.

"Lord, whom did I forgive yesterday?" Listen.

Pause.

After jotting down one or two times you forgave
someone else, thank God for the privilege of forgiving others as you have been forgiven.

*Pause two
minutes.*

Experience says that you are likely to draw a blank
about forgiving others, especially early in the week.
By the end of the week your experience is likely to
be different. Being in touch with the common
everyday forms of forgiveness helps to prepare you
to intentionally love others through forgiveness
when the issues are larger.

Exercise Four: Listening for God's
Guidance for Our Ministry to Others

Pray through your prayer list.

*Say,
Pause three
minutes.*

Prepare for the day's ministry of forgiving love.
Relax, take a deep breath, then let it out.

"Lord, who would you have me forgive today?" Listen.

Pause.

*"Lord, whom do I know who needs to be assured that
they are acceptable as a person?"* Listen.

Pause.

*"Lord, who needs to know that it is OK to make mis-
takes?"* Listen.

Pause.

97

When done, write down the people and acts that God brought to your heart today.

Pause up to two minutes.

Discernment

Say,

As with other aspects of love, you may discover that forgiveness is an easy form of ministry for you. For some, however, it is very difficult. If it is difficult for you, you can use these exercises to strengthen and expand your ministry.

As you ponder whom you need to forgive, remember that forgiving someone is not the same thing as preparing to volunteer to be taken advantage of in the future. Jesus forgave the woman caught in adultery, but also said, "Go and sin no more." God is in the business of transforming lives and uses forgiveness as an agent of change.

If you work for or live with someone consumed with a major addiction (e.g. alcohol, drugs, sex, gambling, abusive behavior or irrational risk-taking), seek help. God will be able to use your ministry more effectively if you learn the difference between forgiveness as a strategy for change and forgiveness as an expression of destructive enabling.

If you know that God has forgiven you, but your life is still run by destructive habits, remember that God intends for you to both stop the old and to substitute a new way of life. Many programs are available to help you learn new ways to cope.

Forgiveness is the foundation of our salvation, but it is many people's weakest ministry. They think forgiveness is holding it in because they want to avoid their own anxieties about confrontation. True forgiveness always requires both honesty and integrity. It is aimed at building others up, not grinning and getting along. Take time to understand, to remember and to practice the type of forgiveness that Jesus Christ offers.

Close with prayer.

Going Deeper

Five discussions on forgiveness follow. Remember this section and read it several times in the weeks ahead. Christ's forgiveness is one of the most difficult things to grasp, and the joyful freedom we gain through it is beyond description.

Day One: Reflection on the Scripture

God takes the initiative. "While we were yet in our sins, Christ died for us." Forgiveness is an expression of who God is. It is not an expression of what we deserve. That is crucial to understand. Having stressed that, the rest of the truth is that others can forgive us for years, but the fact that we are forgiven is useless until we accept it.

Many of us believe that we are not forgivable. We have hurt people we care about. We have thrown away joy. We have avoided and blamed and made matters worse. No matter how much we protest, somewhere inside we know it. At these times even the most positive among us can begin to wonder, "How can someone who has done what I have done be forgiven?"

In these moments we can decide to reject forgiveness and remain who we have been or we can embrace forgiveness and change. Paul reminds us that Jesus came to us while we were "yet in our sins." If we think we do not deserve forgiveness, we are right. The good news is that forgiveness is a gift, not a reward. Embracing the forgiveness of God or others even when we realize we do not deserve it leads to a new freedom. Clearing our souls from the need to rationalize allows us to discover wisdom, to listen to what is actually going on and to move to new possibilities. Forgiveness is a huge new possibility for millions of people.

For Further Thought or Discussion:
- Why does a bad conscience make it difficult to relate to others?

- Paul notes in the second chapter of Romans that we are most likely to give others a hard time when their behavior reminds us of what we dislike about ourselves (Romans 2:1). Do you agree with Paul? Why?

Journal and Share.

Day Two: Hearing Another's Confession

James writes that we are to be prepared to hear another's confession (James 5:15-16). He points out that physical and emotional health and even group viability depend on confession and forgiveness.

We all know that apologizing and accepting apologies is part of any relationship. At times we are in a bad mood, get caught up in our own agenda, just forget to think about the other or misunderstand what is meant. We hurt or offend others, and acknowledging what we did helps clear the air.

If the offense is serious, it is natural to remember why we value the other person and to recall times when the relationship was comfortable and a joy. We seek to restore the relationship and hope the other person values it enough to put their hurt aside and forgive.

We are also aware that we do not deserve forgiveness and cannot earn it. The theological expression is "unmerited grace." It expresses who the other person is and not what we deserve. When we approach the other person, we acknowledge our responsibility, acknowledge the hurt and either implicitly or explicitly promise to change. After all, we do not want to harm the other person again. When forgiven, we are usually grateful and that in and of itself encourages change.

Some people ask for forgiveness with no intent to change. It is a kind of emotional game some people play to gain a supposed advantage over others. In that case, the offer of forgiveness may be authentic, but the request is suspect.

Now let's think about being the one asked to forgive. When another asks us for forgiveness, we are often uncomfortable. We may have done something similar. We may feel uncomfortable being angry with someone we normally like. Seeing their shame may be so difficult for us that we want to rush over the moment. Ironically, though we may be the person who was hurt, we probably have to discipline ourselves to live through the discomfort most of us feel when another has a need to apologize.

The biggest difference between hearing an apology and hearing a confession in the Christian sense is that an apology involves another person and a confession involves God. Confession follows the natural sequence of apologizing. First we acknowledge to ourselves that we hurt someone else or acted against their interests unfairly, even if they do not know what we did. We also acknowledge the discomfort within and that this discomfort is appropriate. Confession does not have to do with what psychologists call "free-floating guilt," generalized bad feelings that are not related to any particular act. Confession relates to actual harm we did or intended to do.

Next, we remember what is valuable in the relationship we have harmed. We then go to the person and tell them what we did and accept whatever questioning, exasperation, anger or sadness they express. We ask for forgiveness. They hopefully give it. We set out to enjoy and enhance the restored relationship.

The Bible teaches that all harm we do others involves God (see Mt. 18:23-35). Many Christians acknowledge that, but many other people, including Christians, do not recognize this teaching. That does not prevent them, however, from time to time realizing that they hurt themselves and others in the same way over and over again. At the moment they take this seriously, they have also discovered that they cannot change themselves. If asking to be forgiven were sufficient, they would be free from the behavior.

Confession ultimately requires us to turn over the management of a part of our lives to God. Even the most committed Christian has this experience. We call Jesus our Master, but reserve part of our lives for ourselves to manage. In confession we bump into the fact that we are doing a poor job of it and need God's help.

To make a confession to God, we recognize our part in harming others, remember who God is and what our relationship can mean, state the wrong and ask for forgiveness. We give control of some part of our lives to God, seek God's leadership and anticipate the future with God.

To hear a confession, we need to understand the importance of each of these steps, encourage the other to address each one and have an understanding of the cross that helps another let go of their past and rely on God.

In the next section I share with you the first time I remember hearing another's confession. If you have never heard a confession, I hope it helps you understand the process. Even if you have done this before, perhaps reading this will help strengthen this aspect of your ministry. Remember, in the Lord's Prayer, "Forgive us our sins *as* we forgive the sins of others (italics mine)."

For Further Thought or Discussion:
- Review the steps in making a confession. Would you add or remove anything and why?
- Review the statement about hearing a confession. What would you add or subtract?

Journal and Share.

Day Three: Carla and Forgiveness –
Turning or Returning to God

The first time I remember hearing another's confession was with a friend named Carla. She had a burning need to know she was forgiven.

When I was about ten, Carla was one of my closest friends, a dark-haired, dark-eyed dynamo. Even as I write this I can see her smile and her flashing eyes. During adolescence we grew apart.

When I was about 20, Carla wanted to talk to me. I had not seen her in about three years. She had become angry. It was as if some malignancy had taken over her soul. She was dwelling on her anger, cultivating her sense of rage and punishing her parents for being so terribly conventional.

"Not like them!" she would say. "I just could never forgive myself for living such a little life. If they died, the Universe would be none the poorer."

That particular day, Carla was sad. Her voice was so heavy I could almost catch her words in my hands. We wandered off to the park we had played in as children.

"What's up?" I asked after a while.

"Jamie," she asked, "do you still believe in God?"

"Yes," I said.

"I need to talk," she replied, then fell silent. We walked some more.

"I have been so angry," she said. "Being a girl was OK, but being a woman is not." She went on for a while. "Because I am angry at life and even at God I have set out to break every rule I could think of. The Ten

Commandments were a lesson plan. I have not actually killed anyone, but I have done the rest. I hoped I would learn not to care about them, about my parents and about God."

She was silent again. She sat down on a large stone by a horse path. Quietly, so quietly, she said, "I failed, you see. I still care about them. I have hurt them over and over again. They get upset and try to be patient and then lose their tempers. The fools love me in their way and I know it. They are not fools, Jamie. I am. They are just people who happen to be my parents. Deep inside, I still believe in God. I am so scummy. What a louse I have been to my parents, my younger sister, to my old friends." She was quiet for a while.

She looked at me and said, "You do not seem shocked or like you hate me."

"Why would I be shocked? You have hardly invented anything new. And even if you had, why would I hate you?"

Carla answered, "I don't know. It just feels like everyone should hate me."

"Well" I answered, "I know how that feels."

"What about God?" she asked.

I asked her, "What have you done that is worse than the soldiers who nailed Jesus to the cross or the one who thrust a lance into Jesus' side?"

"I see," she said. "They really did kill someone. They killed Jesus."

"Yes," I said, "and they probably enjoyed it." She shivered. I asked, "What about the soldiers dividing up Jesus' belonging and playing craps to decide who got his robe? They did it right in front of him while he was dying."

"Oh," she said, "that was really awful. I never thought about that."

"Yes, and Jesus said, 'Father forgive them because they know not what they do.' If God in Christ could forgive them, what have you done that could turn God from you?"

Her face changed. She was visibly surprised. "Nothing," she whispered. "Nothing."

She looked at me and I reached out my hands and stood her up. I asked, "Do you want to talk to God about this?"

"Yes," she said, "but I do not know how."

"You will surprise yourself," I said. I told her I would get her started and asked her to fill in after I became silent. I did that because she had already said in so many words that she felt that she had no right to talk to God. She really did not know where to begin. I used her words as well as I could remember them.

Remembering Who God is: I began with a prayer thanking God for the good gifts of the world, the sun, food, strength, wonderful memories and for being loyal for 3,500 years to the promise made to Abraham. She repeated what I suggested, though she hardly sounded thankful. However, the idea that she had the right to approach God and to remember good things visibly affected her.

Acknowledging the Offense: I then encouraged her to confess to God exactly what she had confessed to me. I also gave her the gift of silence so she could add whatever came to her. I was sure there was more that she had done but was still embarrassed to talk about. I had no need to know.

Asking for Forgiveness: When she looked up from her prayer I smiled and said, "Now ask God to forgive you." You could just hear her say in a tentative whisper, "Father, forgive me even though I knew exactly what I did and why." She looked down like she was about to be slapped and held her breath. She repeated that prayer three or four times until she looked up and opened her eyes and said, "This is real, isn't it? I am forgiven."

"Yes," I said.

Carla looked perplexed. "You know this yourself, don't you? This is not a theory to you. You know this."

"Yes," I said.

Carla then said, "But you have never done anything awful like me."

I understood her confusion. "Carla," I smiled, "I have felt as you feel now knowing that I have hurt people I love."

"What next?" she asked.

Handing over to God What We Manage Poorly Ourselves: "Well, I would offer my anger to God," I said. "There is nothing wrong with anger, Carla. You have just used yours badly. God will help you use it well."

Apologizing Where Appropriate: I added, "Then pray for God to be with you as you go home and apologize to your parents and ask them to forgive you."

She nodded, "Yes, that is what I have to do, isn't it?"

I put my hand on her shoulder, "Yes. After that everything will probably be much like it was before, but I think you will discover that you are free to stop being so angry. You may have to give your anger back to God from time to time, however. It is a hard habit and can take some time to break."

She embraced me and finished her prayer and cried. I felt her go from feeling cold to warm. It was quite remarkable. It was like she was being filled up with warm water. I remember this because it is one of the few times I have actually felt another person as they were being filled with the Holy Spirit, the spirit who comes and cleanses and makes us new again.

A Foretaste of What the Future Can Be: She turned me loose and said, "This is the first peace I have had in years."

Here are four highly practical suggestions. At major turning points people need support. I made a point of seeing Carla about ten days later. In her case, it was time for her to return to school soon. She said that she knew a group of Christian students and she needed to hang out with them. She had already figured out what she needed and where to find it. Not everyone is as proactive as Carla.

When people tell others that they have changed the basic orientation of their lives, they often face skepticism. They are tempted to fall back into old habits. Carla said that it was rough at home. Her parents had forgiven her, but they were clearly struggling. They were trying not to keep on bringing up the past, but were not succeeding that well. I laughed and said that they must be human. Looking startled at first, Carla relaxed and laughed back. Carla was just beginning to learn how to disengage from her own feelings and appreciate those of others. A nudge in that direction was all she needed.

Having been forgiven, everyone needs to practice forgiving others. Laughter helped Carla forgive her parents for being human, but it was still hard for her.

Most people want to know that you are available to them, but they also need some private time. Make sure they know you would welcome a call. If you do not hear from them for two or three weeks, call them.

For Further Thought or Discussion:
- Have you heard another's confession even if you did not call it that?

Journal and Share.

Day Four: Reflections on a Confession

I have gone into detail with Carla's story for a reason. Most people are poor at the ministry of forgiveness. It is a critical ministry that we offer in God's name enabling others to change their lives. When a person is aware of what they have done and why and the harm they have inflicted on others, they often become immobilized by their own shame. They need a spiritual midwife.

And that is a problem. Though confession is completely natural, close contact with another's shame is usually upsetting. We want to change the subject or find a reason to leave. We have to learn to sacrifice our comfort for their need.

No two confessions that I have heard have been exactly alike. However, the need for someone to be there is common. When a person is about to talk about what they are ashamed of, they almost always assume that everyone that hears them will be disgusted. Offering reassurance that "it is not so bad" or "it is just natural" is usually not very helpful. The person probably knows that already.

What helped Carla and many others is to know that they have been heard and understood and that we are still with them, value them and know they can step into a future that is different. Stay with them and remember that our Lord wants them to be free.

Carla's dramatic representation of her sin is common. Recall what Paul wrote about temptation in Corinthians:

> *No temptation has seized you except what is common to man. And God is faithful; he will not let you be tempted beyond what you can bear. But when you are tempted, he will also provide a way out so that you can stand up under it* (1 Cor. 10:13).

Carla realized that her actions were so common that God wrote a book about it. That helped her understand what she already suspected - her lifestyle was really made up of conventional sins that could be overcome.

The Cross is the means of escape from sin. If you are going to help someone, you need to have a theology of the Cross that is biblical, that makes sense to you and that you can share with another. In my understanding of the Cross, one of the things God shows us graphically is that we just cannot do anything horrible enough to drive God away. Carla was helped by the realization that the worst she had done was less awful than what Jesus has already forgiven. What we dread asking forgiveness for is already forgiven. It is for us to grasp the forgiveness, embrace the future and turn to God.

When we are with someone making a confession, we have the privilege of loving that person with the same sort of love we meet in Jesus Christ. We let such people know that we understand them. We value them and know that they can, with God's help, change. As Carla satisfied her hunger to be loved, she could hear God. Forgiveness is powerful.

For Further Thought or Discussion:
- What is the power in hearing another say, "I love you and so does God. You are forgiven."?

Journal and Share.

Day Five: Forgiveness Is an Important Part
of God's Strategy to Change Lives

What we call forgiveness is often a tool for getting along. As such it is
fine, but we need to know the difference between social tools and what
God's forgiveness is actually about.

Socially we say things like, "Oh, don't worry about it. It's not important." We are smoothing things over because we do not want to provoke
an incident. That may be just fine, but this is not the forgiveness we
meet in Jesus Christ. God was not smoothing things over. God wants
change, not smoothed-over poor relationships.

If you read the story of Paul's conversion, Acts 9:1-19, you will see that
God acknowledged the offense. Paul acknowledged the price. He also
acknowledged the gift. God supplied a support group. The result was
change.

Jesus asked, "Why do you persecute me?" (Acts 9:4). This is the oppo-
site of what we do in social situations when we "forgive" people. What
we are really doing is swallowing our irritation or hurt and saying
something like, "Oh, don't give it a second thought." Of course we go
home and give it a second, third and maybe even a twentieth thought.
Nothing is resolved. No one changes.

Christian forgiveness begins by acknowledging the offense. We then acknowledge the cost of the gift.

I heard this story on the radio though I do not remember who told it:

> My son broke the lamp in the living room one night." He said, "Dad,
> why don't you just forgive me? Then everything will be OK."

> I answered him that what he was asking me to do was to pay the
> price for what he had done, then not count it against him.

111

He stopped talking and thought a moment, then said "I never thought of it that way."

Through the Cross, God forgives us and pays the price for who we are. Recognizing the price discourages us from doing it again. Recognizing the gift makes us grateful. Christ's forgiveness is a step toward new life, a life in which we respect others and are grateful.

For Further Thought or Discussion:
- Has another's forgiveness helped you change?
- How does gratitude promote change?

Journal and Share.

Review your week. Share your insights with a friend. If you are in a group, take all your notes to the next meeting.

Week Seven:
Lord, Am I Eternal?

Before you begin: Gather your notes, blank forms and something to write with.

Leaders, provide blank forms.

"Creator God, you who spoke and all that is began, you show such care in even the smallest things in your creation. A drop of pond water is a universe in itself of exquisite beings. Help us to understand how to protect the best in others. Help us know that having been with us each step in our lives, you do not abandon us at the hour of our death. In Christ's name. Amen."

Begin with prayer and pause after each thought.

God loves you. You are uniquely valuable to God, and others simply cannot take your place. God wants to preserve you forever. Some people use busyness as a way of affirming that they are alive in the face of their eventual death. You may be one of them. Being at peace about your death helps you to live at peace during your life.

Pause.
Note: If the group will review the Commitment this session, skip the sharing and Going Deeper section. This creates time to review the Commitment.

You will look at the connection between living as in "living and breathing" and living as in "having influence on the world around you." In your daily cycle of exercises you will focus on affirming the figurative meaning of the word "life," having influence. You will discover that doing this will enhance

113

*Ideally, the group
should have
dinner together
next week and do
the Commitment
then.*

your ministry to others. In the Going Deeper section you will focus on the experience of a realm beyond ordinary experience. Most people are aware
that there is "something more" out there. Many
people describe this sense as a sense of the eternal
Irrespective of your beliefs about eternal life, you
will be encouraged to continue meditating.

The Literal and the Figurative
Meaning of "Life"

*Ask the group to
open their books to
page 114.
Review the
following. If you
are with others,
take turns
reading.*

The authors of Scripture made a connection between being alive and having influence on the living. The figurative meaning of the Hebrew word,
chayah, translated as "life," is "to be lively or have
influence on those around us." The word for salvation, *yeshu'ah,* means to be preserved or saved both
physically and figuratively. On a literal level
"saved" means things like escaping from an auto
accident unharmed. On a figurative level, we save
someone's life when we protect or enhance their influence, ideas, memory or reputation. When ap-
plied to eternity, "saved" means saved from
oblivion at death and saved to a place in the family
of God forever. In the Bible a "savior" can be a person who protects or preserves us from harm like a
doctor, a judge or a soldier. A savior is also a person
who protects or preserves our reputation. That can
include a friend or coworker. Our Savior, Jesus
Christ, does all these things as well as opens the
door to eternal life for us because we cannot do that
for ourselves.

In Biblical thought people who "bear false witness
against their neighbor" are not only trying to gain

an unfair advantage, they are, in a figurative sense, guilty of attempted murder. Gossip "kills" someone's reputation. It is condemned at least 12 times in both testaments. Our ministry to others often involves protecting or enhancing their influence in their family, at work, in the neighborhood and at church.

Jesus used the figurative meaning of the word for "curse" as it applies to the figurative meaning of "life" when he said,

> *You have heard that it was said to the people long ago, "Do not murder, and anyone who murders will be subject to judgment." But I tell you that anyone who is angry with his brother will be subject to judgment. Again, anyone who says to his brother, "Raca," is answerable to the Sanhedrin. But anyone who says, "You fool!" will be in danger of the fire of hell* (Mt. 5:21-22 TM).

Jesus came to give us eternal life. Jesus also came protecting our effectiveness with others and teaching us how to be both as innocent as a dove and as shrewd as the children of this world (Luke 16:1-9). He taught his disciples to protect their time and seek out people who will listen rather than frustrate themselves with people who are not ready to listen (Mt. 10:5-16). The same Lord who came to give you eternal life also came to offer you the possibility of an effective life and calls you to be an agent of effectiveness in the lives of others.

Long before the birth of Jesus Christ the Pharisees concluded that it was bizarre to believe that God keeps promises for thousands of years but walks away from us at the hour of death. God's character is to protect his people individually and as a nation, care for and protect their effectiveness as a culture and as individuals (see the book of Esther, for instance).

The Resurrection of Jesus Christ is the confirmation of what the Pharisees already knew. God is a God of life in all the senses of the word. God protects both our effectiveness and our existence.

The daily exercises encourage you to pray for your daily ministries to others. The figurative meaning of "life" and "salvation" helps you develop your ministry to others.

As you become more aware of how God protects and enhances your influence and that of others, you will become increasingly familiar with God's character. If you do not already believe in eternal life, I am convinced that you will come to the conclusion that God does protect us at the hour of our death. After all, the same God who is actively freeing you from sin and growing you into life is with you at the hour of your death. The idea that such a God would abandon you to oblivion is quite strange.

Preparing to Meditate

Prepare yourself to meditate by taking your center of awareness down from the top of your head to your toes, relaxing each major muscle group as you do. Slow down your breathing. Imagine that each breath that enters is like light filling you, each breath that leaves is like darkness flowing away.

"Lord of Light and Life, clear my mind and open my soul that I might know you. Enter my innermost self. Be the light that is my life. In Christ's name. Amen."

Reread six or so God sightings. Allow the Holy Spirit to move within you to recall where you were and who was with you when you knew that God was alive and with you. Give thanks to God for being there.

Scripture

It is after dinner and Jesus has told his disciples that now is the time that one of them will betray him and another will deny that he knows him.

> *Do not let your hearts be troubled. Trust in God; trust also in me. In my Father's house are many rooms; if it were not so, I would have told you. I am going there to prepare a place for you. And if I go and prepare a place for you, I will come back and take you with me that you also may be where I am* (John 14:1-3).

Say,

Pause three minutes. Pray,

Say,

Pause two minutes. Share. After two minutes, switch.

Say,

Ask the group members to close their eyes. Pause two minutes.

117

Meditation on Scripture

Say,

"If you were a disciple, what troubles would be on your heart?" What comes to you?

It you start analyzing the situation with your mind, pause and wait. Somewhere within your heart another intelligence is at work. If you relax and listen, you will become aware of small tugs and pushes, ideas that sort of shimmer with a different type of energy. Allow the Spirit to address you.

Pause.

"What would you have me grasp?" Listen without effort of control.

Pause.

By now you should have a feel for how to frame this question for yourself. You may feel your way through life. You may sense or intuit. Perhaps you hear the conversation of your heart or see images that will tell you what you need to know. Most people use more than one path. Address your heart in the ways that are natural to you. Empathize with the disciples.

Pause.

"Lord, if I were Mary, what troubles would I feel for my son?" Listen.

Pause.

"If you were Jesus, why would you say these words at this time?" Listen.

Pause.

By relaxing control of your mind, make room for the Holy Spirit.

"In your heart, you are still in the upper room, a room picked by Jesus to spend his last earthly night with you. What would you be thinking, feeling, wondering, hop-

ing, dreading or whatever comes to your mind when you hear your friend and mentor say that he or she is going to leave you alone in order to prepare a room for you in the eternal realm?"

If your mind is wandering, repeat the question to yourself in another form.

Pause.

Make any appropriate notes that will help you re-member what insights came to you.

Pause two minutes, and share.

The Seventh Cycle of Exercises: Preserving Life

"Give me a God-listening heart" (1 Kings 3:9 TM).

Exercise One: Listening for the Truth

Choose partners. Say,

Relax. Remember to pray the phrases of this prayer to yourself as I read.

Pause.

"Lord, will you maintain my existence in the face of death?" Listen.

Pause.

"Lord, is your love stronger than disappointment, be-trayal, loss and death?" Listen.

Pause.

"Lord, will you sustain me even as I experience the diffi-culties of my life?" Listen.

Pause up to two minutes.

After recording what we heard or saw or felt, re-turn thanks.

Say,

As always, be aware that any negative answers you sense are not from God. Make a note of them and learn to pass by them in your thinking. Do not give them your attention or the power to influence your decisions.

Exercise Two: Listening for the Gifts
We Receive

Say,

Relax, take a deep breath, then let it out. Breathe in normally. "Where was I when I experienced your protecting love in the last 24 hours?" Listen.

Pause.

"Lord, where was I when you sustained me in the last day or two?" Listen.

Pause.

"Lord, show me how you have saved what I offered to another from being lost." Listen.

Pause.

After you have made your notes, take time to thank God. It is wonderful to know that even as we face difficult times, we will be kept intact, protected in the sense of being preserved from becoming overwhelmed. In the end you are accepted into God's eternal home.

Pause two minutes.
Ask the group to switch partners.

Share with your partner a time God protected you as a person or your influence in a group.

Exercise Three: Listening for the Gifts
We Give

Relax, take a deep breath, then let it out. Breathe in
normally. *"Where was I when I protected another yesterday, Lord?"* Listen.

Say,

Pause.

"Lord, did I preserve someone's reputation yesterday?"
Listen.

Pause.

*"Lord, did I keep someone's good idea alive rather then
just let it slip by and be overlooked?"* Listen.

How did you preserve another's influence, or protect another from bullying or some other negative
experience? Jot it down because Jesus loved others
this way also. Give thanks to God for our ministry
to others.

*Pause two
minutes then
share.*

Exercise Four: Listening for God's
Guidance for Our Ministry to Others

Pray through your prayer list.

Say,
*Pause three
minutes.*

Relax, take a deep breath, then let it out. Breathe in
normally. *"Lord, is there someone you want me to encourage or protect today?"* Listen.

Pause.

"Lord, who needs to be cared for today?" Listen.

Pause.

"Lord, whom do you want me to cherish today?"

Pause.

Make your ministry notes.

Discernment

Say,

What did the Holy Spirit bring to your heart today? Your notes can serve as a basis for preserving others from harm, or encouraging them or even protecting them from some unnecessary pain. Close your eyes and review the spirit behind each possible action. Only act on those you can clearly relate to God's love. Thank God for each of the people and possibilities that remain on your list. When you are done, open your eyes.

Pause up to three minutes.

This ends the cycle concerning protecting people, their influence and their reputation. To live is to be able to influence the world around us. The God who treasures us and preserves our influence in this life will not abandon us to death. The Resurrection confirms the reality of salvation both as daily ministry and as future hope. As you spend time in God's presence and learn God's character first hand, you are likely to come to the same conclusion. How can the God that loves us in every circumstance of our life walk away from us at death?

The Commitment follows the Going Deeper section.

Going Deeper

There are four days of material this week. They focus on our sense of an eternal realm. Several of them may take you more than one day to digest.

Day One: Reflection on the Scripture

In John 14:1-4 Jesus spoke to both his disciples and to us in simple, physical images. Of death he said, "I go. I prepare. You have a room in my Father's home. I will come. You will be with me." In simple, concrete, familiar images Jesus taught that God protects, preserves and maintains our identity. God does not love our eternal essence or some inner spark. God loves us. Once we are beyond the realm of things, we continue as identifiably ourselves. It is God's joy to preserve us eternally.

Encouraged by Jesus to begin with ordinary physical images, I take a very simple approach to the death of the people I love. I ask for God's help to form a picture of them in heaven.

My parents, for instance, are both deceased. The earthly, physical image I savor of them is one that I recall from a moment when I was about 18. That moment sums up for me what was best in their love for each other.

It was a particularly hot evening in August. I walked in the front door to find an empty house. I headed to the coolest spot, the screened-in porch. I saw my parents in the backyard. My father was in a blue and white cord suit in which he looked particularly handsome. My mother wore a summer party dress with large flowers. They had eaten dinner on a small, round table; the two chairs stood empty.

My parents were standing by the roses. With the crickets singing and the lightning bugs flashing all around, they were embracing in the moonlight. She was in his arms looking up at his face as women do when they have been in love for many years.

In my mind's eye, the moment is not past. In God's backyard in heaven my mother and father embrace. Mother looks up as women do when in love. My father returns her gaze.

For Further Thought or Discussion:
- What persons important to you have died?
- What image drawn from their life might help you remember the best in who they were?

Journal and Share.

Day Two: The Healing Power of Eternity

We are not simply the sum of what we have experienced. We are what we choose to remember and assimilate into our hearts. Many things happen to all of us: the good, the bad and the dreadful. We have a variety of filters we use to process these events.

This image of my parents embracing in God's backyard is one of the filters by which I look at my experience. It colors everything I remember about them. The warm times are enhanced. The tough times are not so important. Life triumphs over death. *"Where, O death, is your victory?"* (1 Cor. 15:55).

Eternity can also help us see the rest of the truth. I have a friend whom I will call Tim O'Shay. He describes himself as an alcoholic, though he has not had a drink in 26 years. Both of his parents drank heavily. His father hit his mother from time to time. His mother had affairs. My friend would say that nothing is free.

Both of his parents are now dead. After his mother's death Tim went to his minister, concerned about his parents' eternal fate. Though both had attended church faithfully and done many good things in their lives, Tim felt that if they truly believed they just could not have been drunks and acted the way they did.

His minister told him to write down everything that God could love about his parents. What in their lives could be celebrated? He went home and pulled out a piece of paper. Three evenings in a row he just sat there in front of the paper and could not think of a positive thing to write down. Then on the fourth night he wrote down, "Mom had nice hair." Two weeks later he had both sides of the paper pretty well filled up.

Tim took his list to his minister. The minister said, "O'Shay, you are not in charge of deciding your parents' eternal fate. That's God's job. If you trust God to do what is right, trust God with your parents. You are wasting your life tied up in what you cannot change. God needs no reminder from you of what was wrong in their lives, nor do you. Thank God for what was right in their lives and let God be God."

"Tim, if you hang on to all your sad stuff you will have to drag it through life. God will allow you to do that. However, it is a waste."

Tim O'Shay told me that he thought at first that his minister was nuts. I laughed and said something about "divine madness."

He smiled. Tim had worked through his initial amazement years ago. After pondering the list he had made, he had begun to see where some of his greatest assets had come from. He came to realize that he had no need to deny the connection between their strengths and his success. He also had no need to dwell on their shortcomings in order to protect himself from the hurt and disappointment his parents caused. Tim's life made much more sense as soon as he acknowledged the rest of the truth about his mother and father. He began to celebrate a memory of playing baseball with his dad and his mother playing first base. In Tim's heart, they play ball in heaven and God smiles. And there were many other things about them to celebrate.

I thank God that all that has happened in my life and in yours does not have the same weight. Junk is not preserved into eternity. When a relationship is ongoing, recognizing junk for what it is helps us avoid needless pain. Once the relationship is over, turning loose of the junk prepares us for new possibilities.

Listen to your past. Find some memory or image of difficult people that summarizes the best. That memory completes the picture of who they are and encourages you to find the freedom to release the hurt and get on with life. A well-developed understanding of eternity helps to free us to live joyful, effective lives.

For Further Thought or Discussion:
- What strength that you value in yourself came from your father? What came from your mother?
- Are you married and having trouble with an in-law? Try asking the question, "Lord, what do I love about my spouse that she/he learned from his/her parents?" What comes to mind? You may still find them difficult, but being in touch with the whole person - both beautiful and not so beautiful - helps. In a sense the exercise encourages you to set your perceptions aside and learn to see people more like God does.

Journal and Share.

Day Three: The Birth of a Child

In this and the next reading I will share several stories that may help you remember moments of "ecstasy" that you have experienced. Moments of ecstasy point to the eternal realm. Though there are other religious experiences that point to a higher realm, ecstasy is one of the most common religious experiences that people have.

There is a short discussion of the various types of religious experience in a book by Howard Rice, the chaplain of San Francisco Theological Seminary, entitled *Reformed Spirituality*.[5] William James, in *The Varieties of Religious Experience*, wrote extensively on the subject.[6]

---

[5] Howard L. Rice, *Reformed Spirituality* (Louisville: Westminster/John Knox Press, 1991) 27-41.

[6] William James, *The Varieties of Religious Experience* (New York: Modern Library, 1936).

As I am using the word, ecstasy is a type of experience, not a designer drug. Ecstasy comes from the Greek meaning "to stand outside of one's self." When experiencing a moment of ecstasy, we are both in ordinary time and space and somehow united with a larger community that is beyond the here and now. This larger community often includes people from the past, the present and the future. Though these words may confuse you, as you recall your own experience of ecstasy they are likely to make more sense.

When my wife was pregnant with our first child, life was difficult for us. I was a young, inexperienced pastor newly installed in the church I was serving. We had no money and we were both terrified that we would do something awful like drop the baby and break it. If you have had a child, you might have gone through something similar.

Being a minister, I am exposed to all sorts of difficult situations including birth defects and miscarriages. I had always had an overactive imagination, but now it was in overdrive. Too much information was not helping.

I would like to tell you about how peaceful our relationship was and how Jesus kept us on an even keel. The truth is that we fought about really dumb stuff, worried a lot and generally made matters much more difficult than they had to be. In spite of our terror at being new parents, God's smile did break in occasionally. Those times were moments of "Wow" and made the rest more bearable.

The time came. My wife delivered our first child, Alexander, and brought him home the night before Thanksgiving. She wanted steak, stuffing and brussels sprouts. After helping her upstairs with baby Al, I came down and fixed dinner. I filled up the tray, went upstairs, and walked into the room. There she was, sitting in a chair having just fed our son. She had that bend of her neck and look in her eyes that just whispers, "Mother." My son had that totally trusting and relaxed look about him of a child just after a meal.

Though I was standing in the bedroom of my home on Wildwood Avenue in Fort Wayne, Indiana, I was also standing there with my father looking at my mother, your grandfather looking at your grandmother, Joseph looking at Mary holding Jesus. Countless generations of men have had their breath taken away by the sight of their wife and first-born child.

That moment did not fix everything, but I knew in a way I had never known before that in spite of all the stress, worries and problems we had run into, marriage and family were worth it. As we went through the difficulties and joys of being parents, I often remembered that moment. When I was so frustrated that I was tempted to give up on marriage and fatherhood altogether, God would call me back to that moment and I would remember to remember the wonder of it all. The memory of that moment kept me going when things were tough. When things were good, and they often were, the memory of that moment filled me with new joy.

I do know where babies come from. I have heard nonbelievers rattle on longer than I care to listen about how our sense of smell is related to why we bond so strongly with our babies and that this celebration of new life give us a survival advantage over species that do not celebrate life. Though that may all be true on one level, on another it is just rubbish! Holding my infant child I knew that the God who is eternal was also with us and had entrusted us with an amazing gift, a new life to nurture.

For Further Thought or Discussion:
- Are you aware of moments in your life that refresh your spirit each time you remember them? If you are comfortable, share one of them with the group.

Journal and Share.

Day Four: Eternity and a Young Atheist Named Marc

Marc was the grandson of a Russian immigrant and a devout atheist. He lived in the same dorm with me as a junior at Brown. He would chide me that I was far too bright to cling to worn out superstitions. I should denounce God and join the Communist Party if I really wanted to help people.

I would avoid Marc whenever possible. I was not worried about his arguments. The truth was that he was simply unpleasant to be around. Most people avoided Marc.

One day I was walking past his room and the door was open. He was sitting in a chair smiling and listening to a recording of the New York Philharmonic playing Swan Lake. He was startled when he saw me come by, then invited me in. I sat with him for about 20 minutes. When the concert was over, he said, "My grandfather was a concert violinist and played that as a young man when it was new music. I can almost see him when I listen. I feel his presence in the music. I barely knew him. He was a very old man and died when I was six. But I remember him. He was a good man."

Marc would not agree with the suggestion that he was experiencing the transcendent in the midst of every day life. He violently rejected the thought that the God who loved both his grandfather and him delighted in bringing them together in some real spiritual sense. When I knew him, Marc would not acknowledge that he had received a wonderful gift, a blessing at the hand of the Creator. Marc rejected the obvious meaning of this experience when he was talking about life.

However, that did not stop him from being caught up in the moment with Swan Lake and his grandfather. He savored it as a saint would. After he turned off the music, he just became "grumpy old Marc," probably a bit grumpier. I left a bit sad for Marc, but deeply moved by the kindness of God who in so many ways allows us to get a small taste of the life to come. God's generosity even extends to the Marcs of this world.

The old Scots have a saying: "Some times and some places are thin so that heaven is but a hand's breath from earth." Marc was experiencing a "thin" moment. Perhaps you have also. If you have had such a moment, I encourage you to accept the testimony of your own experience: God is near, God is active, God cares and God protects us in ordinary and extraordinary ways. God is both eternal and with us. As Paul said to the Areopagus, the group of religious authorities that decided what could and what could not be taught in Athens, *"For in Him (God) we live and move and have our being"* (Acts 17:28).

For Further Thought or Discussion:
- Why do people who have had powerful experiences of the eternal still reject the reality of God?

Journal and Share.

This finishes your final week. I encourage you to work through the questions and if the answers make sense to you, decide to continue to read from the Bible, meditate on in, review your day for God's presence, pray for others and love them with Christ's love. If you are in a group, you may want to have a separate meeting with dinner.

Commitment to Continue

For the last weeks, you have used these cycles of daily devotion. I made you a proposition. Try them out. See for yourself. When you get through, ask yourself some simple questions, then decide what you are going to do.

- "Have these exercises made a difference in how I treat other people?"
- "Am I more aware of God's activity?"
- "Am I more thankful?"

Then decide:

Based on my experience with these exercises, I will continue as a disciple (disciplined one) seeking to develop a God-listening heart. I will use a daily devotional and meditate on the Scripture. I will pray for others and ask God to show me how to love them. As I become aware of other aspects of love that I need to grasp and other areas of ministry that I need to strengthen, I will continue to use this model as a guide to my devotional life. I will meditate at least five times a week for at least 30 minutes a day.

_____   _____
                 Signed   Date

Appendixes

Permission is given to reproduce these forms for personal use by anyone who has purchased this book.

> **Appendix A: God Sightings**
> **Appendix B: Memos from God**
> **Appendix C: Review of Week __/__/__**
> **Appendix D: Prayer List**

The majority of people I work with resist using these forms, but those who do use them find them very beneficial.

Appendix A: God Sightings

Some people object that there is not enough room on the form to describe what happened. Sometimes people say they do not know the result.

I am training you to rely on your memory and the Spirit to recall what is truly important. The more detail-oriented you are, the more difficult using this form will be. From personal experience, the more you want to write the more important it is to be brief. Jot down key words, then practice sharing with others. Try it for seven weeks. You may learn to love it.

As for results, there is a sense in which we never know them. Our lives are always in process. What we do know is that a call was welcomed. We do have a sense as to whether or not we are getting better at saying what we intend. We know if we are hearing what another means or sensing God's leading. Imperfect as our jottings are, make a note. I think that over time you will be greatly encouraged.

Appendix B: Memos from God

The most important thing with this form is to date when you first felt you were being encouraged to do an Act of Ministry, then date when you did it. You will quickly discover that some types of ministry come easily for you and others you resist or even refuse to do. As you ponder your reactions to God's leading in prayer, you will learn a great deal. This is a very powerful exercise.

Appendix C: Review of Week __/__/__

If we do not take time to see the patterns of our lives we are not likely to learn much from our experience. This is an ancient problem. That is why the ancient Greek Philosopher Socrates said, "The unexamined life is not worth living."

Appendix D: Prayer List

If you do not keep a prayer list, here is a form to help you be consistent in your prayer life.

Appendix A: God Sightings

Date	Act/Occurrence	Result

Appendix B: Memos from God

Put the following information on an index card or a piece of paper.

Memos from God: Possible Ministry

Date_____

Name   **Act**   **Date Done Result**

Example: Keep your description of the act short and simple. Note when done. Keep to review each week.

Memos from God: Possible Ministry

Date___2/20/200X____

Name	Act	Date Done Result
Bill B.	*Call about his job search*	
Jane Hare	*Thanks for thoughtfulness*	*2/21/200X Pleasant chat. Husband to hear about promotion in a week.*
Sam G.	*Visit in hospital on way home, or call.*	*2/23/200X Good visit, goes home tomorrow.*

Index cards are good for this. Currently, however, I use a notepad given to me by Joe's Collision Shop. It makes me laugh sometimes as I write down someone's need under the word "Collision." However you record them, these notes come from the results of prayer for God's leading in our ministry to others.

Appendix C: Review of the Week of ___/___/___

Look back over the week's God Sightings and Memos. Pray the following questions:

1. Lord, what are the forms of faithfulness that are easy for me?

2. Lord, what forms of faithfulness are difficult?

3. Lord, how are you leading me to use my current talents, or are you challenging me to become stronger in my ministry by exercising a new or neglected dimension of myself?

4. Are there new areas of my life that I am ready to hand over to Christ?

Appendix D: Prayer List

Group_____

Person & Date	Who Referred and Why	Do I Feel Lead to Take an Action?	Results of My Ministry

Lord, make me an instrument of your peace. Where there is hatred, let me sow love; where this is injury, pardon; where there is despair, hope; where there is darkness, light; and where there is sadness, joy.

Grant that I may not so much seek to be consoled as to console; to be understood as to understand; to be loved as to love; for it is in giving that we receive; it is in pardoning that we are pardoned; and it is in dying that we are born into eternal life.